Hidden Valleys: Haunted by the Future

Hidden Valleys: Haunted by the Future

Justin Barton

Winchester, UK
Washington, USA

First published by Zero Books, 2015
Zero Books is an imprint of John Hunt Publishing Ltd., Laurel House, Station Approach,
Alresford, Hants, SO24 9JH, UK
office1@jhpbooks.net
www.johnhuntpublishing.com
www.zero-books.net

For distributor details and how to order please visit the 'Ordering' section on our website.

Text copyright: Justin Barton 2014

ISBN: 978 1 782799 815 6
Library of Congress Control Number: 2014949212

A CIP catalogue record for this book is available from the British Library.

Design: Stuart Davies

Printed and bound by CPI Group (UK) Ltd, Croydon, CR0 4YY, UK

We operate a distinctive and ethical publishing philosophy in all
areas of our business, from our global network of authors to
production and worldwide distribution.

CONTENTS

Foreword   1

Hidden Valleys: Haunted by the Future   2

Notes   199

For Maysa

Foreword

I had been reminded, by conversations with a friend, about Ryedale and the North York Moors. And a few weeks afterwards I watched two TV plays from 1978 with another friend – Mark Fisher, with whom I made an audio-essay, *On Vanishing Land* – and both of these plays had something that could be described as an eerie aspect, which led to Mark suggesting that an audio-essay of some kind could be made, with the title "Eerie '78." *Hidden Valleys* appeared from out of the encounter between the thought "Eerie '78" and my memories of events that took place in Ryedale, and in the North York Moors.

This book is both personal and historical. But in that it is autobiographical the idea has always been to be "impersonally personal," and its focus is ultimately not on the past, but is contemporaneous, or philosophical.

A fundamental philosophical question is this – What is going on? This is partly the detective question of why human existence is simultaneously so beautiful, and so fraught with violence and horror. But it is also, inseparably, the even more vital question –What is it in the human world to *go on*? (as opposed to being caught in a backwater, going round in circles). *Hidden Valleys* attempts to explore answers to these questions, questions which evidently could not be more practical. Philosophy consists of "outsights" toward the true nature of the world, but as such most fundamentally it consists of means of escape.

The personal aspects are involved because they became valuable for the exploration, and the same is true of the book's historical dimension (which concentrates both on the years from 1975 to 1982, and on the "birth" of modernism around a hundred years earlier, but in the context of the last three thousand years). The aim is to go into the past so as to get to the Future.

1

Modernism is really an eerie *ancientism*. Or to be more precise, an "eerie arcadianism". There is always a wilderness or semi-wilderness: a hauntingly (and hauntedly) positive hinterland, or Outside. And the world of modernism is always transected by an anomalous dimension inhabited by forces that are both positive and negative, and can recurrently prove to be at a higher level of power than the forces of the ordinary world. Ancient Greece has recurrently been involved, but it is evidently not intrinsic – that is, it is not necessary to a specific instance. What is intrinsic to modernism is that it dreams its way beneath and outside the transcendence dreamings of the religions – which means that modernism favours ancient Greece over the ancient forms of Israel and Egypt.

Modernism can be explicit, or it can be a kind of shadow of itself, which carries some of the elements of modernism, but is either a dreaming utilised, and largely destroyed, by a theoretical field (as with Freud and Oedipus), or it can be a mere tracing that creates no new dreaming primarily from the ancient sources, and merely suppresses the power of the existing dreamings (as with Joyce's *Ulysses*).

The eerie wilderness in modernism can be the mountain in *Picnic at Hanging Rock*, or the places by the sea in *The Waves* (both the places by the sea, and the places from which another sea is perceived, in one of which there is an urn at which Rhoda and Louis stand, gazing toward the fluidities of the anomalous dimension). It can be the beach in *Neuromancer*, or the night-countryside emptiness of the places across which the horse-god worshipping boy rides his horse in *Equus* – or it can be Zarathustra's mountains, or a forest somewhere outside Athens, or "the eye of the forest" in Patti Smith's *Horses* (from which you can look up toward "the sea of possibilities").

The wilderness in a modernist dreaming is in fact much less fundamental than the anomalous dimension that transects every-thing – the body without organs, as it has been called [1] – but it may nonetheless be much more in the foreground. Modernist writers enact a lucid awareness of the body without organs, but the exact extent and nature of this dimension tends to be left open. Aspects of the oneirosphere of the human world can be suggested – as with Shakespeare's inorganic beings having a contact with India that does not involve travel in any ordinary sense – but a modernist dreaming in invoking the body without organs lightly suggests its existence, but does not firmly map its extent or aspects.

For blocked modernism in its conventional form the only depth dimensions are sexuality, and the worlds of intrigue and power. The popular counterparts of *Ulysses* are films like *Vertigo* and *North by Northwest* (in *North by Northwest* the protagonist works in advertising like Leopold Bloom, and as with *Ulysses* the film ends with a sexual act, symbolised by the train going into the tunnel). But alongside modernism – and inseparable from it – there is sci-fi modernism. And with modernism in its sci-fi form an extraordinary situation arises. There are no depth dimensions here other than power, intrigue and sexuality (from one angle blocked modernism is cynicism). But it is always the case that there could be alien beings on the far side the wall separating ordinary reality from extraordinary reality (a kind of white wall which is pretending here to have nothing much beyond it). And for instance,, aliens that could have been around for millions of years could take any hard-to-perceive or mutative form that could be imagined.

In the 1950s (a time of sci-fi cynicism, of *The Thing*, and of endless sightings of UFOs) a very extraordinary girl called Barbara O'Brien does the unthinkable while she is at school. She suggests she is capable of the secret crime of "rupture". Society insists that people – and girls in particular – do not start to

3

question, in a sustained, lucid way, across the fundamental religious (oneiric-metaphysical) dreamings and thought-systems of the social field in which they find themselves (on pain of being seen as cold, "graceless" and "un-spiritual" it is insisted that girls go no further than developing interpretations along the lines of existing positions, and never think and dream their way beyond religion, the uses of scientifico-rationality, and the domain of family/conjugality/duty). For her school O'Brien writes an essay about a girl who loses her faith in God, and then reasons her way back to it. Her teacher is shocked, and O'Brien is summoned by the headmaster to discuss this transgression.

And the picture seems to be that later on, when she is working for a big company, Barbara O'Brien turns her extraordinary lucidity and courage in the direction of the white wall, attempting to *see* what could be happening, given that there is nothing but ordinary reality, and given the insistent disturbing aspects of the human world.

The next thing she knows, she is having a ten month, sustained and consistent schizo-vision episode, seeing and hearing a world of quotidian (blandly legalistic and bureaucratic) gangster-like beings who run a gigantic racket controlling human beings, who they refer to as "Things". These gangster-like beings call themselves "Operators" (the title of the thoughtful and measured account of her experience which O'Brien writes in 1958 is *Operators and Things*).

You are left with a feeling that courage and the visionary aspect of sci-fi modernism have thrown Barbara O'Brien very high indeed. The workings of control-mind forces (socially and personally invested forces that are about keeping things "under control" as opposed to them breaking free, and waking up) have the grey, simultaneously gangster-like and legalistic aspect of O'Brien's world of Operators. And it is hard not to imagine these forces thinking "time to push everyone toward mystified love and the road to India – it's getting out of hand, girls are beginning to wake their lucidity -"

Having left behind an unpleasant job O'Brien spends months travelling around America in Greyhound buses – which she believes are run by the Operators – and ends up thousands of miles from where she started, in California, where the schizophrenic episode comes to an end. It is as if the whole experience is a precursor. Just after she has started schizo-seeing the "Operators" (initially she can see them as "fuzzy ghosts" or projections, and later she just hears their voices) O'Brien is told that instead of being operated by an older, stolid operator called Burt, she will now be operated by a young, weird-looking man whose hair she describes – it is 1958 – as "three inches too long."[2] (and with *Operators and Things* what has appeared is a way of seeing the dark-transcendental through the utterly ordinary – an "opening" that will later appear in work such as Pinter's *No Man's Land* and Hammond's *Sapphire and Steel*).

The Beatles invoke love (as well as freedom), and their songs acquire an explicit modernist power by ambient association – there is a wild, dreamy brightness about their music which is a recurrent aspect of modernist works. And as they continue they draw more and more on a surrealist tradition that goes all the way back to that extraordinary modernist, Lewis Carroll. From Alice to Lucy in the Sky with Diamonds –and from "the Walrus and the Carpenter" to "I am the Walrus."

Shakespeare had made a connection to India via ancient Greece (the pre-existing link is that in both cases a whole world and society of divine and anomalous beings is attributed to the body without organs). This is Titania in *A Midsummer Night's Dream* talking about her Indian foster child –

His mother was a vot'ress of my order
And, in the spiced Indian air, by night
Full often hath she gossiped by my side
And sat with me on Neptune's yellow sands
Marking the embark'd traders on the flood. [3]

The Beatles go to India, and at this point for the sphere of songs their work overall becomes an unprecedentedly powerful work of modernism. This "line of escape" (relative to the local dominant religion) carries all of the problems of mysticism and of a different system of religion, and to some extent it will be suppressed by "mother Mary comes to me" in "Let it be" (and later it will come to be less influential than another eastern line of flight – the connection between the modernism of the Beatles and modernism in Japan). But the love-focused lightness of their songs now has alongside it the willingness to dream a way outward (using ancient perspectives) that finds expression in

Tomorrow Never Knows.

However, the Beatles are just one element in an immensely wider process: by the end of the decade a change has occurred in the "western" zone of the human world, no matter how temporary the ruptural aspects of this change might be. Blocked sci-fi modernism has been pushed into the background (*The Invasion of the Body Snatchers* will return, but this is definitely not its time to come back).

There is now a brightness to everything, a brightness that has continued from the early sixties, but which is simultaneously more intense, and more striking through it being in contrast with increasing social ructions and atrocities – strikes, power cuts, the war in Vietnam, the Kent State massacre, Nixon's impeachment, etc. The brightness is to some extent evoked by the view of Solaris from the space station in Tarkovsky's 1972 film. At depth it is an awareness of there being another, much better form of existence that could be reached if the intent was impeccable enough – it is a view toward the Future (the Future that was there all along).

Modernism has now been inflected by science fiction to a large extent, but its eerie ancientism is unchanged. The planet Solaris is to be envisaged as having been around for a very long time, and it is nothing if not eerie. A little earlier there was *2001, A Space Odyssey*, with its culminating invocation of the lightness of "becoming-child" as fundamental to reaching maturity – the eerie, ancient-and-modern world of *Thus Spoke Zarathustra* gets the last word in the film, through the figure of the child, and through Richard Strauss's *Also Sprach Zarathustra* (Nietzsche's book states that the vital "metamorphosis of the spirit" is going from being "a lion" to being "a child" [4]).

And the fictions, or dreamings, that are not in any sense science fiction recurrently either involve ancient wildernesses – or Ancient Greece etc – or they consist of oneiric critique, which display disturbing depth-aspects of the human world (these are

7

often modernist by virtue of the fact that they and their context suggest a dark-transcendental direction that has nothing to do with the dark elements in the blocked dreamings of the religions). Pinter's *No-Man's Land* (1973) uses the language of the ordinary world to produce an impression that something darkly enigmatic is being figured by the play. Whereas Shaffer's *Equus* (also 1973) explores the idea that something fundamental is being left behind in the modern world, and does this this by creating a connection to ancient Greece (the reason for modernism drawing upon the ancient world is not really to dream of a time that pre-dates the extant religions, but is primarily to make contact with an oneiric, planet-focused lucidity). Dysart (the doctor) in *Equus* speaks out for a dreamy perception of things and spaces as so beautiful the affirmation involved becomes in some sense transcendental:

"I wish there was one person in my life I could show. One instinctive, absolutely unbrisk person I could take to Greece, and stand in front of certain shrines and sacred streams and say 'Look! Life is only comprehensible through a thousand local Gods.' [...] And not just Greece but modern England! Spirits of certain trees, certain curves of brick wall, certain chip shops if you like, and slate roofs...'"

[...]

"... in the morning, I put away my books on the cultural shelf, close up the kodachrome snaps of Mount Olympus, touch my reproduction statue of Dionysus for luck – and go off to hospital to treat [Alan] for insanity"[5]

It as if something is being seen that has to do with love, and with freedom, and that is not about Gods, or anything anthropo-morphic, but which instead involves currents that run through existence that are unseen by the 'brisk' eyes of entrapment within ordinary reality (eyes that refuse to be entranced).

The most intense point of this whole phase is probably 1975, when the film of *Picnic at Hanging Rock* appears, an exceptionally eerie and positive film (it is very close to the book, written in 1968) which suggests that three women characters have gone into a wilderness and have crossed a threshold of existence, so that they have disappeared from the ordinary world (the ancient is emphasised by the pan pipe music, and the transecting anomalous dimension is invoked by the opening, "all that we see, and all that we seem, is a dream, a dream within a dream"). This is also the year of Patti Smith's *Horses*, an album which was probably to some extent inspired by *Equus*:

> ...Johnny gets the feeling he's being surrounded by
> Horses, horses, horses, horses
> Coming in in all directions
> [...]
> In the night, in the eye of the forest
> There's a mare black and shining [...]
> I didn't waste time I just walked right up and saw that
> Up there – there's a sea
> Up there – there's a sea
> [...] a sea of possibilities

But also, it is around this time that Stephen Donaldson starts writing his "strange tale" or "second world tale" *The Chronicles of Thomas Covenant, the Unbeliever* (a trilogy, it would be published in 1977). Donaldson – who was at Kent State University when the shootings occurred – has reached for the most effective form available (although it is hard one to use well), and this story is remarkable for its haunting wildernesses, its evincing of the anomalous dimension, and its inclusion of elements from many ancient traditions, from the worlds of ancient Scandinavia and Greece to those of indigenous American peoples.

Donaldson is not a horror writer, despite the fact there is an immense amount of very disturbing horror in these books. And in opening up a view toward the anomalous – the transcendental – in a positive direction he is now increasingly working against the tendency of the time. Stephen King in writing *The Shining* (also published in 1977) has a boy with an enigmatic word appearing in his dreams. In *Equus* Alan cries out the word "eck" in nightmares, and no-one knows what it means (it is the beginning of the name Equus). And in *The Shining* Danny has nightmares in which he sees the word *REDRUM*. The movement forward of the alternative or modernist culture is being prevented, and as energy is being depleted the focus gets more taken up by the process of looking in the direction of the dark-transcendental: the attention of modernism is now shifting toward an exploration of what might be haunting the human hotel.

But a question is this: is it necessary to reach the *singular* – and the impersonally personal – to answer the riddle of what exactly are the intent-currents that make up "love-and-freedom," as opposed to "control"? And a second question is – looking with a perspective toward the eerie, what was happening in the "western" world in 1978?

3

I loved the Black Swan Hotel, and I felt strangely *at home* there, in a way that I could never have put into words; I loved Helmsley, where the Black Swan looked out over the gently south-tilted market place – Helmsley, tucked serenely into the most secluded place in a near-circle of hills; and most of all I loved the North York Moors, whose presence was right at the heart of my love for the hotel.

The North York Moors are an expanse of long ridges running north to south from a wide, ridge-plateau, a heather covered summit-land that extends east to west for fifty miles. The ridges are part of what forms a long series of hidden-away valleys, sun-favoured, carved out by glaciers that could not cut nearly so deeply into a five-mile deep (forty mile wide) wall of harder rock before the vale of Pickering to the south, so that the rivers of the valleys all force their way out through tiny steep-sided, forested windings of hills, with all of the roads going high alongside these narrow outflows, then dropping down into a hidden dale. Bilsdale, Bransdale, Farndale, Rosedale, Newtondale...

I had lived there, in two different villages, as a young child, and then I had lived in New Zealand for nine years. And maybe the distance turned out to be more powerful than the proximity could have been. When I returned from New Zealand, aged 15, my mother's stories about Yorkshire had set me up to dream my way past ordinary-reality half-perceptions, and to see the compelling beauty of these high hills, and secluded valleys.

And the moors seem somehow to cast a glow, or a glamour, across the rolling hills that stretch down twenty miles to the town of Malton, and across the woodlands and villages of the Vale of Pickering, the vale (the floor of a post-glacial lake fifteen thousand years ago) which has Malton as its south-west corner, and which has the river Derwent flowing through it, a river which flows westward, away from the coast.

It was October, 1977, when I returned from New Zealand. There were odd parallels between the radical, "there-is-another-way-of-living" alternative culture of that time, and what was happening in my life. My own radicalism was my being determined to stay out of school. I had not been at school since I was eight, and seven years later – having spent the time running wild and reading books in New Zealand – I was very much committed to remaining free. I had had almost no contact with punk at this point, but the ABBA song I had really loved was SOS – and it was this song from which a guitar riff had been taken for "Pretty Vacant," the third single released by the Sex Pistols. Later, in 1985, I would be at Coleg Harlech, an adult education college in North Wales, and friends with Nial Jinks, who was the first bass player from the post-punk band Scritti Politti, and was living in Harlech, and the fact I had never heard of Scritti Politti, or heard any record by them, never got in the way of us being friends (music in some ways is as much about the dreamed futures it comes from and inspires, as what it is in itself). For me what was about to arrive at that time was an extraordinary year of living in hotels all across England and Wales, though mainly in Yorkshire – while my mother was ostensibly disputing her father's will, and while she looked for a place for us to live – followed a few months later by a year working for very low pay in a village shop (there would then be another year, in total, of living in hotels in the years immediately afterwards). For the leading-edge worlds of the culture around me what was about to arrive was a final phase of the twenty year wave of alternative-culture intensity that would be marked by the emergence of fictions and songs of striking new kinds, and that would take place across Margaret Thatcher's election victory in May, 1979. (Aged 14 I had already worked full-time for five months when myself and my sister – who would not return for another four years – had been left on our own for a year in New Zealand, but with this there had been the joy of independence from parental authority, and of it being a covert activity, in that according to the law I should have been at school. However this was 1977, and like the general election the change of circumstances was far in the future).

* * *

There were many hotels – too many for me to easily remember them all. But alongside the Black Swan there was the Talbot Hotel, in Malton – an old, quietly attractive hotel, around a corner from the market place, and on a slope looking out toward the countryside across the River Derwent. I loved the Talbot, but in comparison to the Black Swan the beauty of the hotel and the place were somehow more challenging, less reassuringly serene.

At the Talbot, in the spring of 1978, I read *The Shining*, having bought the book from a stand in the foyer. I read it through the night, terrified by the trips I was forced to make to get to the toilet at the far end of the hotel corridor (opposite the toilet was a bathroom with a claw-foot bath, just visible in the darkness). I probably finished it at 4 in the morning. Reading the book had been unexpectedly unnerving, but I was very impressed by it. I was struck by the corridors that stretched back in time as well as space; by the quotation at the start from The Masque of the Red Death; by the way in which the boundary between dreams and reality becomes blurred as the Overlook "wakes," and most of all by the way in which Danny is split between an ordinary self and a futural self called Tony, who is trying to help his "younger" form (the feeling is that Daniel *Anthony* Torrance has developed a more capable self, under pressure from extreme circumstances).

Looking back at that year-long phase of living in hotels there is an elusive eerie quality, which primarily has a *sunlit-eerie* aspect. The eerie is here to be understood primarily as an awareness – however fugitive it might be – of unknown forces that could be either positive or negative, and that are both "out of sight" around you, and could perhaps in some sense be stalking you, or moving closer to you. But the *sunlit-eerie* is something different, and is to do with the feeling that the transcendentally unknown is there, in front of you, and that this direction is the beginning of the real adventure.

But this second feeling – which came most from being in countryside, or from reading books – was fugitive in my experiences, in the sense that I just inspired myself with it, but kept it at the non-objective remove of seeing it in terms of feelings and fictions, rather than attempting to follow the line of awareness that was involved. Even the isolated, rare events that now appear as eerie – or even as gothic, in one case – did nothing to disturb this stance.

In my first year at Coleg Harlech (the college which turned out to be my way of getting to university, given I had succeeded in never returning to school) I set out one day to capture the atmosphere of the times when I had stayed at the Black Swan. I had just read for the first time about automatic writing, and almost all of this was written within the space of half an hour (I gave it the name "Haven in Winter"):

And long and down through the clocked corridors
On quiet carpets I carried my books and wondered
At soft spines of leather, and crisp, shining leaves.

The smoke of gold, bright and morning-windowed
That drifted on sleeping days of sunset beauty
Was the cold that warms the memory when you turn away to
    warmth.
And often, more than often, I turned with that shining
And took the amber glow down the corridor within me,
The gently padding corridor, clocked and soft,
With windows only on snow and winter slumber

Of dark hot beech trees with frozen sparks of leaves,
Still brightly hanging, and telling of last year's fire.
Warm and rich as buttered toast and jam
By a blazing mantled fire when snow is falling
Slow and deep, the corridors and passages I wandered long
   and then.

Came spring and the fading crimson bindings brightened
Like the robin, and disappeared among the leaves
That burst bright into vital green. Only to dry and fade
So quickly. The wood in the darkening grate burns out,
The ashes it leaves grow cold, and their greyness
Is the daylight of a wet June day without shelter.
The crackling of a dying fire grows louder like the clocks
Of the warm lamp-lit corridors that amplified their music
Into harsh news of parting, and the hard glaring stares
And spaces, of the world beyond a dream.
The long dream of haven's doorway, and of coloured perfect
   warmth
Beneath the blanket of the snow's wide eaves.

And long and down through the clocked corridors
On quiet carpets I carried my books and wondered
At soft spines of leather, and crisp, shining leaves.

Part of what is eerie about this poem is that it displays a fear of
summer (which here should perhaps have its full abstract sense
of "life at the highest available level of intensity"). This is
coupled with the fact that the protected place – with its clocks,
and where the leaves of trees have been replaced with the leaves
of books – feels like a place of disguised entrapment (you are sad
to go, and it can be wet in June, but all along it was a trap). The
sinister aspect of the "haven" is established through the faint
predatory suggestion of "the gently padding corridor;" through

it being a winter place; and through the connection to the world of The Shining (the clock is a fundamental and menacing feature of the Overlook hotel, and the phrase "I turned with that shining" makes the connection more explicit).

* * *

Perhaps the most eerie event during that year was a striking dream that took place at the Talbot, also in the spring of 1978 (it would have been around a month after reading The Shining). One night I dreamed that I was learning about a community of people who had lived in a high valley in the equatorial Andes thousands and thousands of years ago. The community lived in a smallish town in a steep sided valley, and upstream of where they lived they had constructed a dam, making a reservoir lake that supplied them with water (I should say that I had not started reading ancient history at this time, and that I never managed to connect the dream with anything I had been reading or thinking).

I knew that the community was extraordinary: its people were warm, inspired, lucidly creative. They had been at an exceptionally high level of spiritual and intellectual development. And by this point in the dream I was *seeing* everything at the same time as being told about it. Like a lived experience that somehow retained something of the quality of a documentary, although it was far more intense, and charged, than a documentary.

A voice said, telling me what had happened:

"One night it rained, and rained..."

I was standing on the side of the valley, in extremely heavy rain, above the town, and downstream of it, but with a view back up the valley. And in the darkness I saw the dam break, and I saw a wave of water come down the valley and sweep the houses away.

The sadness of the dream was heart-wrenchingly intense. They had been so wonderful – kind, inspired and visionary across an unknown threshold of awareness and lucidity. And they had been destroyed. They had been destroyed by unprecedentedly heavy rain under the cloak of darkness – *and by their own energy supply.*

Looking back now – rightly or wrongly – I experience this dream as a breaking-through of something fundamental, both historically and contemporaneously, about the entire human world. In what way has the human energy supply (energy of lucidity, creation, dreaming-of-futures) been turned against itself? What is this ongoing war-torn Disaster called human history?

And did that dream come from the Future (life at a higher level of awareness), rather than from the past?

* * *

And returning to the starting-point, what is this place – the North York Moors; Helmsley, Malton, the Vale of Pickering? A place of hidden, secret valleys that lead into a vale which itself is hidden away by hills from the plain of York. A place of wild gooseberry bushes in tiny wooded valleys, of larks, bracken, granite-buttress hills, tiny villages, wild strawberries, wild raspberries, high hill-roofs of heather. A place hidden away, and relatively un-sung, out of the spotlight; an area that was defeated three times (in 1066, in the Wars of the Roses, and in the Civil War) and which has been left to dream unencumbered by romanticising poetries and fictions.

I had been back in this area once before – over from New Zealand in 1970 for three months with my sister (and toward the end with our mother as well). We had stayed in Pickering, on the edge of the moors, fifteen miles east of Helmsley, initially with the family of a friend of my mother, who was called Patricia Brandon.

I was eight years old, and it was a sunny day in early summer.

We had been dropped off at the end of a tiny lane running down a hill through woodland. Me, my sister, and Mary Brandon, the 18 year old daughter of the family. We were 8 miles north of Pickering, and we were going to walk south down the Newton Dale valley along a derelict railway line.

At one point we turned off the railway line, and walked for a while through an area of woodland, on a footpath. Mary said "I always think it's like Narnia." I knew what she meant because around a month before I had read *Prince Caspian*. I was immensely happy – because I had loved the book very much (it had been the first genuine dreamers' book I had read – the first book to "blow me away") and I was now talking to a kindred spirit, and also because I loved *Mary*, and it was very exciting to have something special between us (I remember saying, when I was around 6, that I wanted to marry her).

The woodland, the sunlit, forested valley with its derelict railway line (it is always easier to see the planet when the human things in the terrain are derelict), Mary, a strange-tale "dreaming." In one day three fundamental intent-currents had been heightened a little within me – through a moment which had involved all of them.

Women.

The Planet.

Dreamings.

The intent-current of dreamings would rapidly go into full, intensifying effect (I had no 'peer group' to tell me what I should or should not be reading, and given I was not at school I had plenty of time). These are some of the books/stories that had a profound effect on me over the next 8 years: *The Chronicles of Narnia; Alice in Wonderland/Through the Looking Glass; A Christmas Carol, Jane Eyre, Beau Geste* (P.C.Wren); *A Dream of Armageddon /The Door in the Wall/The Time Machine* (and many other stories and novels by Wells); *The Call of the Wild, A Wrinkle in Time* (Madeleine L'Engle); *Interview with the Vampire* (Anne Rice);

Watership Down; The Shining.

The intent-current of the planet went into effect in the form of my intense fascination with what gets called "the weather" (it could also be called "the sky"), and in the form of my desire – enacted as much as was possible – to go straight off into any encountered area of hill-land, mountains or semi-wilderness.

The intent-current of women had been crossing a threshold over the year before the dream at the Talbot. I had been yearningly attracted to a girl called Astrid when I had been working in a shop in New Zealand. I bought Astrid a scarf as a birthday present (she was 18, and she was about to get married). And around the time when I had the dream at the Talbot Hotel I was "in love" with a 16 year old girl called Colleen, the sister of a woman who worked at the hotel, who was visiting (I only had a few conversations with her, and then she returned to her home, in Lincolnshire).

* * *

And with the dream about the people in the Andes, a fourth intent-current had to some extent been glimpsed – the Group.

But the full arrival of this intent-current only took place later. Around 15 years afterwards (having never been back to the North York Moors area) I started having a series of dreams about an extraordinary group of friends living in a house in the middle of a forest a few miles from Malton (a forest which is always there in the dreams, but which in non-dream reality does not exist).

These dreams are an interesting story, and have a curious connection to the writings of P.C. Wren, contemporary of Virginia Woolf, and the writer of one of the only works in the list of books, from earlier in this section, which has no straightforward "fantasy" elements.

Another story is the eerie beauty of the times I spent staying at the Black Swan hotel over the next three years, and the story of the books that I read while I was there, books that were always extraordinary, even though they all had problematic aspects. This in turn would lead to a description of the experience I had of meeting a hidden world of "inorganic beings" on the only occasion when I took DMT: an experience that ended with me walking (south, toward the front of the building) through the long, warmly charismatic corridors of a windowless version of the Black Swan hotel.

Lastly, in 1978 it seems perhaps that something new is emerging at the level of "affect" and of ways-of-being in relation to established systems of power. A second memorable event for me was in the early summer at The Talbot hotel, when I was blown away by watching *Once Upon a Time in the West* (a film from 10 years earlier). I was 15, and full of light-hearted optimism, and I felt that what I had seen was someone whose life was shaped by a worthwhile intent, a charged, vital plane of consistent action. But I was perhaps slightly more aligned with cultural developments than would have been discernible from the date of what I had watched, and from my extremely minimal knowledge. Out in the oneirosphere those last few warrior-spirited dreamers still standing – in the end-phase of western-world proximity to the Future – were apparently all coming to a conclusion: *there are circumstances in which only coldness will keep your love alive.*

4

No new "dreamings of escape" have arrived. No new female-oriented abstract-oneiric worlds have emerged that would help people dream their way out from the religions, with their primacy of male Gods, male deity-incarnations and male manifestations of "supreme" or "divine" consciousness. The film of *Picnic at Hanging Rock* was three years ago. And it is also three years since both *Black Moon* (a film in which a female character crosses a threshold into the unknown, and does not return) and Pierrette Fleutiaux's powerful tale, *The Story of the Telescope and the Abyss*, which culminates in a transition to freedom that causes ordinary reality to collapse, in that it becomes clear that it had been an illusion. The liberatory joy and dreamers' lucidity of The Beatles – with the becoming woman that runs through genuine hetero-male love songs – had come to an end at the beginning of the decade. And – again – it is three years since Stevie Nicks' invocation of the Welsh sorceress Rhiannon:

> She rings like a bell through the night
> And wouldn't you love to love her?
> She rules her life like a bird in flight
> And who will be her lover?

(Gilles Deleuze shows an awareness from the outset of the new phase, in the early 60s – as in his 1963 essay "The Mystery of Ariadne According to Nietzsche" - that the whole modernist escape-path is utterly dependent upon the waking of "becoming-woman" and the creation of liberatory dreamings about female explorers of the unknown[6]).

There is still the *haunting brightness* in the background of everything. The feeling that the Future is close is still there for anybody who starts to dream and think in new directions. And yet at the same time there is a pervasive insistence of all forms of reactionary, control-minded traditionalism. An insistence made more sinister by the fact that cutting-edge zones of religio-political "controlism" are now decking themselves out to as pro-woman, anti-racist, etc.

It is as if "jolts" have started to take place for those whose form of life is centrally about the creation of dreamings. An atmosphere of struggle starts to appear, although it simultane-ously involves a heightening of awareness, in different ways, of what people are struggling *toward*. Ursula Le Guin, the very great writer of anomalous tales, says this –

> I gradually realized that my own fiction was telling me that I could no longer ignore the feminine. While I was writing *The Eye of the Heron* in 1977, the hero insisted on destroying himself before the middle of the book. "Hey," I said, "you can't do that, you're the hero. Where's my book?" I stopped writing. The book had a woman in it, but I didn't know how to write about women.[7]

And it is at this time that P.J.Hammond dreams up *Sapphire and Steel*, a TV series that becomes something far stranger than was initially envisaged.

The two protagonists are "investigators" who attempt to discover and fend off intruders from another dimension – from outside what is called "the time corridor." In a series of abandoned, or near-empty places (a house, a disused railway station, a closed-up shop…) they use anomalous knowledge and abilities to navigate in the face of the radically unknown (Sapphire is one of the first female figures of this kind since Dunsany's Ziroonderel, from 1925). They are dispassionate in their responses, displaying a de-subjectified poise which appears as a necessary attribute in their struggle against coldly controlling, destructive entities. In the process of these struggles apparently ordinary elements of human existence (nursery rhymes, clocks, paintings, photographs) are re-seen as strange and disturbing, and the two investigators are threatened by claustrophobic traps that are not in any ordinary sense 'spatial' or 'concrete'. At the end of the final episode they are permanently caught in one of these traps.

Entrapment is also a central theme of *No-Man's Land*, which in 1978 was filmed for TV, with extraordinary performances by Ralph Richardson and John Gielgud: this is in part because the characters in the play give the impression that they have all been trapped by a mode of being which is fundamentally about power, and whose lightness of tone is all along an expression of a will to impose upon others around them to the maximum extent. The extreme insouciance of these people is a dark coldness, a playfully imperturbable and unembarrassable state that is evidently dispassionate, but is for the purposes of holding sway over circumstances.

The *Invasion of the Body Snatchers* has now come back, in the form of the impressive 1978 film. But this modality of oblique social re-perception is manifested far more strikingly by the 1978 TV drama *The Ice House*, whose vegetal, parasitic entities display a serene pleasure which they maybe also transmit to the human beings with whom they form a dominating relationship (one that has an aspect of symbiosis only if it is forgotten that although the human victims have pleasure, they have neither love nor lucidity).

After 1978 oneiric critique to a great extent expresses itself in a series of stark warnings. The feeling is of it having been seen that the human world is a disturbingly haunted hotel, and of an urgency in suggesting the extreme difficulty of the struggle that has all along been taking place. New pervasive conservatisms and manageralisms are just around the corner – but this will just be a more constrictive expression of the underlying problem.

In the film of *The Shining* Jack Torrance kills Halloran

(Halloran survives in the book), as well as being destroyed by an incursion of something monstrous lurking within the Overlook. Only a woman and a cat survive the coldly predatory directives of the corporate controllers of the Nostromo, in *Alien*. In the final episode of *Blake's Seven* all of the crew are killed by "the Federation", the corporate-imperial world they have been fighting. Sapphire and Steel are caught in a trap – a denuded and claustrophobically enclosed space – without any hope of escape. Meanwhile, George Smiley in *Tinker, Tailor* senses something suavely nightmarish – an engorged, ethereal control-craft – at work everywhere within the eerie mists of the true libidinal England that is perceived by lucidity.

And in France the writers of *A Thousand Plateaus* suggest that if people really saw what was going on behind the fabric of ordinary human existence they would be likely to scream in terror[8]. And more than this, they take their analysis to the point where it includes both love and sexuality, as well as issues of constrictive, pathologically blocked abstract perception. They encode into their title the extraordinary question, "do you have enough coldness (and *love*) to not only become, but to *not come*?" (the concept of a plateau was developed by an anthropologist called Gregory Bateson who used it to refer to "plateaus of intensity" attained by certain tribal practises of avoiding being trapped within the up-then-down of "coming" [9]).

But of course, it should be said that *this* form of being imperturbable in the face of attacks and impositions – disguised attacks in the form of false claims upon your time and affection – is all along the hot coldness of extreme poise: it is love in full effect, as opposed to the control-fixated coldness of the characters in *No Man's Land*.

* * *

It is early January, 1978. We have arrived at the Black Swan. It is the first time I have stayed there, and I am already being swept away by the atmosphere of its small ancient downstairs rooms with their blazing fires, and its many corridors and staircases, and Elizabethan wood beams, and steep, oval-shaped Georgian stairwell, and its long, varnish-scented modern extension at the back. We have come up from spending two weeks in Devon, in a slightly bleak hotel in Newton Abbot, where I have been watching a series of poignant but un-compelling sci-fi films. Everything is now suddenly bright, warm, lucid – a feeling of being woken up into serenely real dreams.

It is a cloudy, wintry morning. My mother had obviously made the booking in advance, because I remember that when I arrived at the table in the dining room for breakfast there was a letter on the table to which I was shown which had been sent to the hotel from my sister in New Zealand.

The Black Swan is three buildings that have been run together. Looked at from the market place a half-timbered Tudor building is on the left, alongside trees on the edge of the churchyard. Then there are two quietly beautiful buildings which are probably both two hundred and fifty years old. Going back from right-to-left, the long series of tiny lounges culminates in an unaffectedly ancient lounge with diamond-paned windows (whose panes have flaws in them, revealing them to be extremely old), and a narrow, cosy TV lounge set down three feet below the ground-level of the churchyard alongside it. You would sit facing the TV, which was placed in front of the north wall, in an atmosphere which was recurrently friendly, like being in a living room, alongside the bodies in the churchyard – what better place to watch the TV dead?

The hotel is a fused world of time-pockets, in a perfect place at the top of a market square – which in turn is in a small town hidden away in the middle of some exceptionally beautiful countryside, the moors rising immediately to the north.

Through the window in the dining room I see that it is

starting to snow. It will be a small snowfall, only an inch or so, but the next day there will be a heavy fall, followed by bright, frosty sunlight. Let your point of attention drift – out through the dining-room door, and out through a small unassuming front door into the falling snow of the market-place: go half-way down the cobbled square and look left into the window of a gift shop where there is a poster in the window called Close to the Edge (later I will buy it and send it to my sister): a bright blue lake whose surface takes up the entirety of a sheer-sided plateau, with water pouring down the towering cliffs on all sides, a lake-plateau, high up in a light-suffused sky.

5

Early summer, 1978, at the Talbot Hotel. It is afternoon, and I imagine it was a Saturday or a Sunday, and I am in the TV lounge, and I find myself watching *Once Upon a Time in the West*. It came from nowhere, appearing from out of a space – the Western – from which I expected only atmospheric cheap thrills and glory dreams (in this sense a glory dream is always vacuous and/or sentimental, and is often deeply pernicious). Also – I had seen very few films, and almost no good ones.

In the film I saw a life-transforming, tightly-focused *intent*. An intent which was in fact really the intent to become a free, maximally active and defended being – a "warrior."

During the day or so after seeing the film I felt challenged, brightened, and affected by a new longing – a longing to have a genuine *purpose* in my life. I also felt an urge to act with courage, and to leave behind pettiness and neurosis.

At some point in the days before I had been shouted at by the hotel gardener for climbing over a fence from a field into the hotel vegetable garden. Outside the main entrance of the hotel was a small parking area, but to the left there was a balustrade above a ten foot drop to the garden, giving a strikingly wide and evocative view of the River Derwent curving through the valley two hundred feet below, and – in particular – of a south, wold-countryside horizon consisting of a hill-line several miles away and of outlined trees and small copses (the effect of this view on me was always to make me dream of losing myself in beautiful, enigmatically compelling countryside beyond the horizon). The day after the film I was standing looking at this view, with the gardener working thirty feet away, in the garden below me. I remembered the film, and responding to its challenge, I plucked up the courage to apologise to the gardener for endangering his fence and plants. The gardener cheerfully accepted the apology, but the outcome was not really the crux – the key issue was that the film had taken me a tiny fraction in the direction of a disciplined way of being which has no fear of mockery or derision.

Once Upon a Time in the West is quietly a very powerful, radical film. The protagonist is in fact an indigenous Native American Indian (perhaps originally from what became Mexico, as opposed to America), as is revealed by the actor who plays him as a child. The horror of what happened to this man's brother – and to him – is a place through which can be heard a kind of seismic howl of the agony of the crushed indigenous peoples of the Americas. But instead of "Harmonica" being a stock figure of suffering for hand-wringing liberalism, he instead becomes a view (a little obscured it is true) toward a state of being that is utterly beyond and above the forms of existence that together make up the social systems of the new countries of these continents.

The way in which the view of the warrior state-of-being is obscured concerns the fact that harmonica's concrete "mission" can only be characterised to some extent as revenge. Even if the goal is now simply to rid the world of a monster, the structure of the act is that of revenge, with all its inciting power, and, crucially, it is also true that an approach to the goal involving a whole series of other deaths in fact has no quality of the "impeccable" about it. In the sense in question, a warrior's intent is to travel toward love, freedom and wider realities – revenge is not one of his or her motives.

A fascinatingly contrasted tale is told in one of Castaneda's books: Castaneda states that Don Juan – a Mexican Indian – recounted a similar event, involving a brutal hacienda manager who tricks and works to death the Indian "peons" who work for him, and he says that his own teacher told him that the process of overcoming a "petty tyrant" is an extremely valuable challenge for honing and focusing a warrior (this honing and focusing is in fact fundamentally about losing self-importance), should they be lucky enough to have a petty tyrant of this kind available to them

[10]. But the overcoming of the petty tyrant is here about causing them – simply by finding ways of calmly avoiding attacks – to fall apart into a self-destructive rage, and is not at all about setting out to kill them, let alone about revenge (although with petty tyrants at this level of extreme brutality it is quite possible that they will end up dead in some way as a result of their immolatory collapse into rage). In the interests of losing self-importance, and without feeling any hatred, it is a process of causing the petty tyrant to give way to anger to the point where they lose their power (whatever form this loss of power might take).

At the end of the 20 year phase of greater proximity of the Future there is the appearance of the prepossessing idea of coldness. Or, to be more precise, the idea of the different manifestations of being *dispassionate*. And it is important to see that there is always a lightness and laughter on the part of those who have focused this attribute. With the full, positive form it is recurrently a *bright* twinkle in the eye, a look of humour, that is also a look of warmth. In the control fixated or control-ensnared form there is something that is better described as a kind of dark twinkle in the eyes- the look, for instance, of all the characters in the 1978 adaptation of *No Man's Land*.

To be dispassionate is not to be deprived of something. On the contrary, it is to be immeasurably heightened, as a result – as pointed out by Spinoza – of having been freed from the deeply draining storms of passions, or *passivities* [11] (the functioning in yourself of something that is not really your own will). Love is not a passion, and nor in itself is laughter (although there is a dark passion in the form of irony), and love and lack-of-graveness are fundamental for an escape toward the Future.

In 1978 the western world's oneiric-abstract climate is growing colder. And therefore the dispassionate heat of the warrior (the freedom from the passions) is becoming urgently necessary. The fundamental struggle is overcoming self-importance, but there is also an increase now in those who police the death queue of collapsed, capitulatory existence – those chilly, judgemental individuals whose impositionism is a re-imposition of normality. For such individuals there is the calm of a high degree of success in relation to most passions, which does not perceive the passion of its domination by a fixation on control.

As everything becomes colder, it is not surprising that actual coldness becomes a primary subject matter, along with the apparent coldness (the quiet extreme heat) of those whose dispassionateness is free, unenslaved.

6

I wrote this in September of 2013, around six months before getting the idea for this book.

The summer of 1978. The Future is close. If I went to the top
    of a fell
In the morning with the right girl – in love with her -
It is plain that we would see the Future.
The spring was Wuthering Heights, and Blondie -
Denee, Denee...

(Kate Bush was born as the Future
Was about to arrive, in an ancient farmhouse time-pocket
In what recently had been Kent – the building surrounded by
    a large orchard
A wooden fence, and an expanse of new suburbs).

I have returned from ten years of friendless non-school
    freedoms
In New Zealand to friendless hotel nomadism with my
    mother, in England
And Wales, though mostly in Yorkshire – a strange, disjointed
    nomadism
Of searching for a house to buy, or rent – punctuated
By visits to solicitors about a contested will, and by long
    diversions
Inspired by my mother's love of different areas of the island.

It is June, and for the first time in eight months of wandering
My mother has failed to book a hotel, and instead we are
    staying, wonderfully,
At a farmhouse bed-and-breakfast on a sun-facing hill

At the head of Wharfedale, between the tiny villages of
    Hubberholme
And Yockenthwaite.
That morning there had been a gigantic row in York
About me taking my New Zealand bicycle, against my
    mother's strong objection
Out of a Pickfords warehouse tucked just inside the city wall
Leaving us with a bicycle that for weeks I would ride between
    hotels,
And which the rest of the time would be awkwardly jammed
    across luggage
In the back of my mother's estate car.
(once I cycled from Ripley to Grassington,
and through a thunderstorm on the pass before Bolton
    Abbey).

It turns out the owner of the house is a bright-minded woman
From a city somewhere, probably in her late thirties,
Intellectual, and artistic by interests – though maybe not an
    artist.
The house is beautiful, sparsely but brilliantly decorated.
In an upstairs hallway I am blown away by Rousseau's
    painting
Of the lion in the desert trying to wake the sleeping musician.
(The next day I will walk across a fell and a valley to Pen y
    Ghent
Entranced by the fells, but aware of aloneness.
One highpoint of the day, after walking twenty miles is the
    kindness
Of a woman who I see outside a farmhouse
Emptying an ashpan, and who gives me a pint of orange
    squash, when I ask for water.
At one point I run three miles to attempt to catch up with
    some walkers

With whom I had been talking until I discovered
I had left my coat behind).
That evening I talk with the woman, who I think was glad of
some company.
She has been reading a book called something like "The Long
Walk"
About a gruelling walk south through Siberian forest
After an escape from a gulag. I am being warned against a
thought-trap
On the path to the true radical escape – one which, because I
am not at college,
Has had no chance to catch me.
A few years later the widespread depression from the
collapse of the belief
In this false outside, through full awareness of gulag horror
Will be one element in the slipping-away to the far distance of
the Future.

Two days later I cycle off down the valley
Bright with sheer youngness,
The youngness that is the recurrent unconsidered joy
Of a wide now and dreamed astonishing futures.
And if I had known that it was all true
But that I was a fabric of illusions about when I would reach
These places, and their surface details,
I would not have cared at all.
But the last illusion within such exuberance
Is that it does not matter.
Nothing matters more
Than our certain eventual death, and the fact we have no time
For the diversions of self-indulgence (the something-
happening of being consumed
By a passivity, by a will not our own),
Or for those other passions, the fear-fuelled slumps and

drifts.

Soon the Future will be receding, closer only in the
countryside.
Kate Bush will maintain contact for *The Hounds of Love*
Only by leaving for a studio at the Kent farmhouse
And for westward doorways to the bright, sensual Outside.

* * *

In 1977 Stephen Donaldson's *The Illearth War* is published (it is
the second book in the late 70s *Chronicles of Thomas Covenant*
trilogy, and it is the best of these three "strange tales"). And in the
story two extraordinary figures appear, and then are destroyed.

There are five figures moving in a landscape of mountains,
four of them on horseback – they have been drawn away, by a
new event, from a war that is taking place in a country called "the
Land" (an eerie arcadia on a vast scale). The first new character is
a woman called Elena, who is best described as a "warrior-
sorceress," and who is the main leader of her people (which
overall is led by a group of – male and female – guardian figures
of the same kind, who are called "Lords") as well as being the
daughter of the protagonist, Thomas Covenant, who comes from
the ordinary world. Elena's task is to save her people from a
malevolent entity called "the Despiser," and her specific danger
is that she will not be dispassionate enough in relation to the
passion of hatred.

The second new character is a laughing, entirely dispassionate
being, who is a little reminiscent of Puck in *A Midsummer Night's
Dream*. He is called Amok, and like Puck he has the form of a
human, but is not in fact a human being. What it seems is lacking
in Amok concerns the fact that his nature is intrinsically to serve
another person's purpose: he has existed, roaming around the
world for several thousand years, but at a specific signal (set up

by his long dead creator) he has to fulfill his function. It should be added at this point that the other two figures on the journey also foreground the theme of "dispassionateness": they are members of an ultra-ascetic cadre of martial arts exponents called "the bloodguard" whose original vow of service to the Lords had the unanticipated result that they remain alive without ageing until they are killed in combat.

Thomas Covenant – a novelist – has contracted leprosy, and for several months has been living in an isolated house in the country somewhere in the mid-West of America, having been abandoned by his wife, and separated from their young son, because his wife is afraid their son will catch leprosy. He is suddenly thrown into an experience of being in another world, apparently by a mysterious Creator figure, with this experience starting after him accidentally walking out into an oncoming car and blacking out.

Having arrived in the other world – which is immensely beautiful – he is encountered and greeted as a hero-figure by a young woman called Lena. Covenant, who in the ordinary world must check his extremities continuously because leprosy has destroyed his nerve endings, does not have leprosy in "the Land" (Lena gives him a salve that cures him) and decides that he must be going through a crash-induced wish-fulfillment hallucination, and also decides that it would be deadly for his ability to survive back in the ordinary world if he were to give credence to the existence of this second world. Caught up in sensorially-heightened events shortly after meeting her, and with the non-excuse of his sense of reality being destabilized, Covenant rapes Lena. The horror of this act – from a protagonist who until then has shown himself to be bleakly anguished, but sympathetic – is part of what gives a believable quality to these novels.

In *The Illearth War* Covenant returns after a few weeks back in the ordinary world: but in the Land thirty five years have passed, and the Lords are being led by Elena, who is Lena's daughter from the rape. Covenant is now the same age as his daughter, who is an immensely poised, warm, but broodingly fierce figure. A war is starting with the army of "the Despiser", but in the midst of the onset the enigmatic Amok appears. He turns out to have been made by one of the "old Lords" who, on the brink of a cataclysmic defeat, has made Amok as a guardian of something called "the Power of Command" such that he will appear when the leaders of the Land have returned to a level of knowledge that will allow them to use this power. Amok's puck-like nature is given in the entirety of his brightly playful, dispassionate affects, and also by passages such as this – when asked where he has been he says "I have feasted with the *Elohim*, and ridden sandgorgons. I have danced with the Dancers of the Sea [...] and traded apothegms with the Grey Desert [12] (there is an earlier reference to "the sylvan faery *Elohim*"). Together Elena and Covenant set out into a mountain wilderness, led by Amok, to reach a labyrinthine place deep beneath a mountain, at the centre of which there is a spring whose water will – very briefly – give the Power of Command (the spring is like the door in *Stalker* – it will turn out that for unknown reasons even Amok's maker never came to the place and drank the water). The affect-complexity during this journey is extraordinary – Elena is in love with Covenant, and Covenant, who feels extreme guilt toward Elena's mother, is nonetheless being drawn toward the woman who is his own age, but is his daughter.

Briefly, in 1977, a warrior sorceress appears – in a powerful, sustained dreaming that has a very extraordinary body without organs (the Earth here is sacred, and is very definitely hypersubstantial, or Spinozistically substantial in an explicit, populated way). She appears, and then is destroyed.

In what feels like a repudiation on the part of Donaldson Elena's fierceness is made to be a weakness in the form of an anguished fury – a fury which, when allowed to express itself, will disastrously abandon sound judgement. It as if an awareness of the passions involved in fighting will only surface in fantasy when a fierce warrior woman is envisaged. It is in the strongest sense necessary to critique fighting in the form of violence in favour of fighting to escape from constricted reality, but this is not a critique of violence, and appears more as a bias against women ("don't allow the woman to fight"). The misogynistic oneiro-metaphysics of this trilogy is sometimes minimal and recurrently not in effect at all (it is not generally as grotesque as it is in C.S.Lewis's anti-sorceress world where the only evil central characters are female) but it nonetheless inflects the whole dreaming. The mysterious Creator figure who has thrown Covenant into another world is male, and although Donaldson allows Elena to become head of the Lords, it is also the case that with only one slight exception all of the epic "hero" figures of the distant past of the Land are also males. There are many very extraordinary, positive aspects of Donaldson's trilogy, but there is something disconcerting about such a striking sorceress figure appearing and being killed-off so rapidly, and about her being both the daughter and virtual lover of the male protagonist – as if such a figure could only appear in a form where she is maximally tied to a "heroic" male (Covenant is not yet at all a "hero", but of course inevitably, at the end of the trilogy that is what he will become). Also, the male dispassionate state is being implicitly constructed as lacking in fundamental ways (the "bloodguard" are portrayed as sympathetic, but they do not laugh, have love relationships, or initiate action, and the picture of the non-fighting Amok is that he has lived a life of dalliance, waiting passively to fulfill his programmed purpose) and the gender counterpart of this is the implied suggestion that the female dispassionate state is all along prey to emotions that would make it dangerous in a warrior.

The laughingly dispassionate Amok dies when they reach their goal, and Elena dies after commanding the ghost of the man who made Amok to attack and kill "the Despiser". This ghost entity is defeated, and is hurled back in a state of insane rage to kill Elena (at the end of the third book it is discovered that the Despiser can only be killed by laughter). For many hours Elena fights against this ghost (we do not see anything of the fight, not even its ending: the description is of its sounds and distant tremors, as Covenant's protector bloodguard Bannor drags him forcibly away, to save him). In the blackness of the underground labyrinth, after half a day of fighting, Elena is killed, and this disturbing virtual-real event of 1978 has ended.

To get the full eerie effect of this death it perhaps needs to be added that although Ursula Le Guin creates a whole series of sorcerers in the late 60s and 70s she never creates a sorceress, and that Sapphire three years later will also reach a dark, claustrophobic end (permanent entrapment in a room-sized space).

* * *

In 1978 there is the first broadcast of *No Man's Land* (October 3rd, 1978). This play is a world of chilly, insouciantly "playful" dispassionate individuals (with the persistent feeling that its subject matter may not entirely be the world of the human, but might in part be a terrain – as in the work of William Burroughs – of dangerous "inorganic beings"). They are the sophisticatedly control-fixated; those who live in "No Man's Land", or on "Bolsover Street":

Briggs
"He asked me the way to Bolsover St. I told him Bolsover Street was in the middle of an intricate one-way system. It was a one-way system easy enough to get into. The only trouble was that, once in, you couldn't get out. [this is followed by a series of intricate directions] ... All he's got to do is reverse into the underground car park, change gear, go straight on,

and he'll find himself in Bolsover Street no trouble at all. I did warn him, though, that he'll still be faced with the problem, having found Bolsover Street, of losing it. I told him I knew one or two people who had been wandering up and down Bolsover Street for years. They'd wasted their bloody youth there. The people who live there, their faces are grey, they're in a state of despair, but nobody pays any attention [...].[13]

One central character seems to be dying. He is called Hirst, is perhaps a successful writer and critic, and is definitely an alcoholic. What follows is the very end of the play, which seems to be his death, a prefiguring of his death, or perhaps some other form of collapse that stops short of death, a collapse even more disastrous than going straight on in the underground car park and arriving in Bolsover Street:

Hirst
But I hear sounds of birds. Don't you hear them? Sounds I never heard before. I hear them as they must have sounded then, when I was young, although I never heard them then, although they sounded about us then.
Pause
Yes. It is true. I am walking towards a lake. Someone is following me, through the trees. I lose him, easily. I see a body in the water, floating. I am excited. I look closer and see I was mistaken. There is nothing in the water. I say to myself, I saw a body, drowning. But I am mistaken. There is nothing there.
Silence.
Spooner
No. You are in no man's land. Which never moves, which never changes, which never grows older, but which remains forever, icy and silent.
Hirst
I'll drink to that.

He drinks.[14]

There is something about this passage – this ending – which lifts *No Man's Land* completely away from other works of oneiric critique, whether compared with previous works by Pinter, or with most things in the books of Burroughs (or with the films of Kubrick which concentrate on the problem of human worlds of power, such as *Barry Lyndon*).

* * *

In Ballard's *The Unlimited Dream Company* – which he was writing in 1978, and was published in 1979 – there is also a character who may well be dying. The protagonist – Blake – crashes a stolen plane into the Thames at Shepperton at the very beginning of the book, and perhaps the most compelling reading of the book is that all its events after that are a death-generated hallucination on the part of a concussed pilot drowning in the river.

This book attempts vastly more than is attempted by *No Man's Land* – as is signaled by the central character being called Blake – and in many way it falls far short of the goal, leaving you with the impression that Ballard is straining on the edge of a full abstract-oneiric perception.

Blake has a coldness that lies in him not being at all neurotic. But he also has an insane, dominatory aspect (the control mind in an extreme form) which exists alarmingly alongside him being a "visionary" with an adventurous, implacable determination to free himself and everyone else from their attenuated lives. As Shepperton begins to melt into a world of tropical birds and plants (which seem to have emerged from Blake's imagination), where people can fly, and can metamorphose into animals, Blake in his mind becomes explicitly the centre of a kind of cult of libidinally hypercharged freedom (with very little love involved, it is mostly a kind of sensual-perceptual phantasmagoria). However, in the end, Blake does get "woken up", in a culminating process which involves a striking – and very moving – intervention by animals to save him after he has been shot in the chest and left for dead by the people of the town. Saved by the animals, Blake goes on to save the people of the town from their entrapment within "ordinary reality", and then sinks down into a collapse which seems inexplicable other than as a sign that it has all been a post-crash death delirium which is now coming to an end.

Ballard has set out to look toward the Outside – using the lens of a heightening dispassionate state on the part of Blake – but instead of a system of oneiric outsights there is primarily only an importing of anomalous metaphysical ideas, and of powerful words and phrases, without a consistent "spiraling upwards" of the story. So that its success – if seen as showing a death delusion on the part of a quite unpleasant human being – also feels in part like a kind of pre-determined failure. Overall it seems that what is most eerie about *The Unlimited Dream Company* is the clash between where Ballard is looking, and the choice of a character who initially is largely a kind of "empty shell". The book becomes a chaotic space of glimpses taking place within a primarily control-dominated trajectory of action (which when it is no longer an expression of the control mind, at the end, is undermined by it mostly having a depthless quality that suggests a delirium created by total collapse).

* * *

Then there is the TV drama *The Ice House* (December, 1978). This is a world where the "dispassionate" entities are vegetal, centuries old and parasitic on humans – but in a way where they free humans from all human neurosis and anguish.

These non-human beings apparently have a manifestation which has the form of a female human being, another which is a male human, and a "core" manifestation which takes the form of a climbing plant which has male and female flowers (operating from a fake "health spa" country house, they also have an ice house which they seem to use for "acclimatisation", in a process of transforming human beings into mobile elements of the plant entity). The striking thing here is that the victims seem, perhaps, to reach a point where they live a life of continual low-key happiness – a kind of calm vegetal "joy".

However, in fact joy is far too positive a word, and because of the absence of love (or perhaps it could be said that this is degree zero of love) this world of dispassionate existence is indeed a world of horror.

* * *

Again – in yet another domain of production in 1978 – Deleuze and Guattari are more than half-way through the seven year process of writing *A Thousand Plateaus*. And the precursor cold of the collapse-back to lower intensity has now begun to make itself felt. Francois Dosse, in his biography *Intersecting Lives*, characterizes the year before – 1977 – as "the year of combat" [15]. He describes how it was at this point that the "new philosophers" started – with the aid of the French media, and using reactive moral concepts – to attack all philosophers with radically liberal, and anti-establishment views . However, this onslaught was set up to be genuinely successful against many "leftist" thinkers – and spuriously successful against Deleuze and Guattari – because it included within it an urgently valid attack on communist Russia's standing through an exposure of the horror of the gulags. It is no wonder that the very dispassionate Professor Challenger in "The Geology of Morals" says to his audience "we have to hurry" (the third section of the book is an abstract tale, a description of a lecture by this figure). Later Guattari will characterize the decade after 1980 as "the winter years" (to re-employ Pinter's title from his 1982 play, "a kind of

Alaska" is arriving…).

However, the real struggle all along is elsewhere, and Deleuze and Guattari in 1978 have reached a terrain consisting of an ability to see the spaces and forms of intent at work within the human world (one which in no sense needs to be left behind as a result of a predominant falling back from the Future). What they are seeing is partly the body without organs in the direction of Love-and-Freedom, and is partly those elements or forces within the body without organs that make people experience "winter" when this need not be happening (if they only were to wake up, and embody an escape-journey).

Something contingent or "attached" (not at all our own will) has been pre-programmed into the organism that we are in relation to reproduction, and onto this stratum of passivity another totally different stratum has been imposed in the form of the endemic system of blocked thought – and reactive moods and behavior-modes – that can be described as "the control mind." Deleuze and Guattari are aware that human beings – unless they have broken free of ordinary reality – are fabrics of passions, of imposed modes of feeling and acting (passivities).

* * *

And lastly – what is behind the thinness of the voice of Cathy in Kate Bush's Wuthering Heights? (March, 1978). The quality I have in mind is when Kate Bush sings "You know it's me, Cathy", and "I'm so cold" (as opposed to the fey, ghost-dance quality of "out on the winding, windy moors"). It is the opposite of the situation with No Man's Land. With the inhabitants of Bolsover Street there is the energy necessary for life, but without love. As if Kate Bush has tuned herself to the last moments of a lover's life, in the song Wuthering Heights instead there is love, but there is not the energy necessary for life.

Stand by the Talbot Hotel looking south toward the hills across the valley of the River Derwent (think "filmically" for a moment, but with the mind's eyes reaching out for a gigantic back-story).

A part of the southern fringe of the Vale of Pickering is just visible to the southeast, below wolds escarpments; to the west there are hills into which the river disappears. It was here where, 10,000 years ago, there was the outflow of the large, glacier-fed lake which had what is now the "Vale" as its lake-bed. Later the lake remained, after the glaciers, and human communities lived by the lake. At the level of the human socio-religious world, it is now around 1000 years since the last societies flourished in this area whose religions included a belief in goddesses, the remaining vestiges of these beliefs perhaps having been brought to an end by the massacre referred to as "the harrowing of the North", in the winter of 1069, when it seems around 100,000 people were slaughtered (though this was a brutal response to a rebellion, rather than an attack for religious reasons).

At the level of the Planet, everything has been heating up for around 18,000 years (with a large number of species having been lost to this area recently as a result of human activity). But fundamentally at this level there is an immense, unfilmable sky of flows and vortices of air, there is a river, with its "tributary" streams and rivulets, and there is a plain surrounded by a complex terrain of hills, wolds and moorlands.

* * *

These are the first dramatised fictions that really "struck" me – that haunted me, set me thinking.

1977 *Summer of '42* (1971)

1978 *Once Upon a Time in the West* (1968)

1979 *The Go Between* (1970)

1979/80 *Equus* (BBC Radio dramatisation). (Play written 1973)

1980 *Dersu Uzala* (1975)

The fictional books that first made a strong impression on me had been written over a much longer timespan, with the span beginning around the middle of the nineteenth century. But here everything is compressed – everything has been made in the space of eight years.

There is no science fiction in the list, even though I loved science fiction, and had seen a few science fiction films (I had enjoyed sci-fi films, but nothing had really inspired me). I am certain I would have been strongly affected by *Solaris* and *Stalker*, but for me they were both still around fifteen years in the future.

Taking these dreamings for a moment as a single entity, they have two frontiers, one to the west, where the indigenous North American social worlds are being destroyed, and one to the east where the people of the Siberian hunter *Dersu Uzala* are also being swept out of existence, along with many of the forests of their terrains. In terms of societies that do not conform to the structure of the modern state, there is a thematic link to ancient Greece through *Equus*, and there is a direct connection in relation to *Dersu Uzala* and *Once Upon a Time in the West*.

The list is probably more valid through me having had no peer group (throughout the time involved) to influence me, but at the same time it is of course highly contingent, given that, although I watched a quite a few films, my film-watching was nonetheless both random and sporadic.

The films as a whole show you a very diverse, beautiful, dangerous world of "outside" spaces. And they also seem to be revealing perturbing aspects of sexuality and love relationships, while showing there is something equally dark at work within the relationship between the western world and the societies beyond it.

But also – it is as if modernism's dreamings have arrived in new constraining circumstances, cut off from the world that *initially* had been seen, at some time in the decades before the Second World War. There was once a West (the translation of the title of Leone's film): there was once truly an outside that was visible. The line to the past has been cut – on the far side of it are *The Waves, The King of Elfland's Daughter, Thus Spoke Zarathustra.* Tracing the change through at the level of critique, the main emergence of modernism had seen it growing up alongside religion, and leaving it behind by dreaming its way to the ur-world of the Spinozistic intensity-cosmos, in a process that simultaneously showed up the strange world of reactionary figures who argued against Darwinism, women's' equality etc.

But the connection to the past has been cut in the sense that the forces primarily pressing on modernism, are now, firstly, the dull, numbing, but highly effective forces of "scientifistic" concrete-world empiricism, and secondly, the equally misleading and draining philosophical overcodings of figures such as Kant and Freud (Kantianism overcodes the transcendentally unknown-but-knowable as the unknowable, and Freudianism overcodes love as sexuality).

The whole modality of fiction is to reach the outer edges of the abstract through dreamings, rather than to argue with philosophy, so now fiction has something pressing upon it from what is in fact a lower level of abstraction, and whose dreams cannot, in passing, be focused and unblocked, simply because what is pressing upon it has no dreamings – that is, apart from the denuded dreaming of the billions-of-years-long history of the cosmos, with its tendency to take attention in the wrong directions. It feels as if, as result of the new circumstances, a harking back is taking place to a time of greater lucidity before the Second World War. *The Go Between* goes back to the summer of 1900. *Dursu Uzala* (a joint Japanese/Russian production) is based on a

Russian memoir written in 1923. *Summer of 42'* is an American film based on a "yearning for something lost" 1971 memoir of events at the very start of US involvement in the Second World War. *Once Upon a Time in the West* goes to the 1900s.

Meanwhile, Doctor Dysart in *Equus* is yearning his way back all the way to Ancient Greece. This is an instance of the wider search within the past for lucidity that is characteristic of modernism (and inseparably it can be pointed out that something which leaves behind the attenuated line of ordinary cosmos-history is a process of exactingly "dreaming up" what has been taking place in the last 12,000 years in the human world and the surrounding planet – something which is attempted by *A Thousand Plateaus*).

The list of dramatisations being considered here is extremely small, but there are other "breakthrough" films from the time which fit with this picture. Picnic at Hanging Rock (book, 1968, film, 1975) is also set in the summer of 1900, like The Go Between, and Black Moon (1975) is principally inspired by Alice in Wonderland/Through the Looking Glass. These films are made at an exceptionally propitious, high-intensity time, but they suggest, nonetheless, that it was valuable (perhaps only in a talismanic sense) for them to have a connection to the first phase of systemic modernism, in order for the film to be swept up by the intensity.

* * *

Why did I love these hills around Malton? Why did the area make me dream, and make me feel so much that I was in the right place? It is not that I had any shortage of beautiful areas for comparison. On the contrary, my mother's bizarre trajectory of hotel-nomadism involved lengthy stays (or whole series of visits) to various regions of the Yorkshire Dales; to Northumberland; to the Lake District; and to the far west of Wales (the west of Dyfed, or what was then called "Pembrokeshire").

The area is not only hidden away, it is also quite inconspicuous. For what it is, it is relatively unfrequented: the most famous moorland in England is in Devon, and the North York Moors are not obviously singular like the limestone terrains of the Pennines.

But perhaps as important is the fact that this area has a relatively large number of trees. It is a terrain of woods – they are not large forests, but from the moorland-edge valleys and all across the Howardian Hills to the areas around Malton there are always many expanses of woodland on the horizon.

When fifteen years after leaving it I started having the series of dreams about the area, it was this aspect that was accentuated.

* * *

In the first of the dreams there was a forest – seen from above – that stretched across the "Howardian Hills" northwest of Malton, and into the flat area of the "vale" to the east. And in all of the other dreams there was a forest covering a large area of hills starting four miles to the southwest of Malton, on the opposite side of the river from the town (an area of hills which I have never visited).

In the centre of this second forest there is always a largish house, reached up a woodland track, where a group of friends are living (in the first dream there was also a house in the middle of the forest, and the overall details and atmosphere of the dream were the same). There is an extraordinary brightness and warmth about these people: their lives are collectively about travelling into the unknown across thresholds of existence (although it always feels as if the process of escaping from ordinary reality has only just started – as if the group has been based there for only a few months, or maybe a year). In relation to the place and the circumstances the atmosphere is "I can't believe we've made this happen," and the feeling is that the house is a practical, matter-of-fact – but very beautiful – domain, which is a base from which journeys of different kinds are made (rather than it having the quality of a dogmatic centre, shut away from the outside world).

In at least two of these dreams I knew that the house in the forest belonged to a woman called "Patricia Brandon". But this woman was a "dream fusion" of a woman called Patricia Brandon in the P.C. Wren novel *Beau Geste*, which I had read when I was ten years old ("Lady Patricia Brandon" who has a large house in the countryside in Devon), and my mother's friend from Pickering who had the same name. The woman in the dreams in fact was a contemporaneous figure (she had a serenely strong quality about her), but she was slightly reminiscent of both of the other women (one from a book, and the other from my past), and shared their name. The impression she made was that she would have had an affinity for an inspired, creative life of familial and conjugal warmth (like a modern Mrs Ramsay, from *To the Lighthouse*), but that instead she had taken her warmth in the non-bourgeois direction of becoming a traveller into the unknown.

Percival Christopher Wren wrote *Beau Geste* in 1924. In the world of this novel there is a man who is utterly in love with Lady Patricia Brandon – who has been in love with her for many years, while mostly living overseas – but with no chance of having a relationship. To use an antiquated term, it is "courtly love". And what brings everything together here – so that something new becomes visible – is this idea of being in love, but without being in an enacted sexual relationship.

With the group of friends – women and men – who live in the forest it is intrinsic to the feeling of the dreams that there is a very intense love and comradeship between them, but without this love being definable at all in terms of sexual relationships, no matter, in some cases, how dispassionately and blissfully *amorous* it might be. In *Beau Geste* Patricia Brandon is in an enduring "courtly love" relationship. With my mother's friend Patricia Brandon (who I never met after the age of eight) there was a child's very real love for a kind, bright woman who for at one point acted for several weeks as "a mother" - a love without sexuality as any sort of apparent element. And lastly, with Mary Brandon (who by association is involved here) there was an eight year old boy's genuine, yearning love, but a love without any obsessiveness whatever: and although in a strong sense this love was amorous, it was also without any apparent sexuality.

The first three intent-currents to "arrive" were the planet, women and dreamings – when I was with Mary Brandon, aged 8, in a forested valley of the North York Moors. A fourth intent-current signalled itself at the Talbot Hotel, twenty miles to the southwest, and seven years later: the group.

But now the fourth intent-current begins to come into focus, and with this dream of friends living in a forested terrain there arrives a fifth:

Being in love, but intrinsically without sexual acts.

8

The Black Swan, Helmsley – January, 1978.

A day after the light snowfall, a much heavier fall. My mother and I walk four miles on footpaths through fields, traversing a bright upland of snow, walking from Helmsley to the ruins of the old monastery of Rievaulx, a kind of gaunt, beautiful sombreness, hidden away in its valley. But it was the forested countryside covered in snow, and the ultra-bright sunlight, that together entranced me that day. I had been in love with snow since I was 8, but in Christchurch in New Zealand snowfalls are rare and minimal.

It was when I was at the Black Swan, that first time, that I have my first memory of something that became a recurrent mode of "envisaging": when I was on my own in a hotel room I would imagine I was on a space-ship on an inter-stellar journey and that the room was a computer-generated projection designed to give me a calming environment. I would then be in a "modern" hotel room in a building whose Elizabethan part always seemed to predominate in the overall impression it gave: and this brightly-modern-but-ancient space was being envisaged as a kind of capsule hallucination created by a spaceship community in deep space, which had voyaged away from Earth, but which was using "virtual-real" Earth worlds to assist with the strain of being in deep-space.

I know I did this relatively often in those years in hotels, though looking back now it is mostly the rooms of the Black Swan that I remember, and the memories have taken on a striking colouration from a dreaming from eight years before that time. There is something genuinely eerie about the final few scenes from *2001: A Space Odyssey*, a film I did not see until ten years later (however, during a stay at the hotel that summer I read and was – to some extent – impressed by Arthur C. Clarke's novel, *Imperial Earth*). An interesting point about this recurrent element of "sci-fi" living was that I did it as a kind of calming joy: a reversal in relation to the state imputed to those on the spaceship. For me what was calming was the idea that I was in deep space, and that everything around me was insubstantial – was the body without organs.

On another occasion at the Black Swan, either that summer, or another time two years later, I also remember focusing closely on the fact that, as I was going to sleep (and in fact to some extent *in order* to go to sleep) I would recurrently imagine that I was in a spaceship – accompanied by a kind of disparate, non-human crew made up of a speaking computer and chilly but reliable and companionable robots – and that I was being pursued by a small group of enemy spaceships across gigantic interstellar distances, with my process of escape manoeuvres always involving faster-than-light travel through space-time "worm-holes". (I remember thinking – doing this one night at the Black Swan – how strange what I was doing was, all along...)

What could it mean that it was *soothing* to me to imagine I was involved in a hyper-charged life-and-death attempt to evade malevolent pursuers? Was it because it was soothing to have everything in perspective before confronting the "dark" of sleep, valuable to perceive my true circumstances? (perhaps this could even be a starting-point for thinking about what is eerie about human existence as a whole).

And also – what kind of techno-Prospero is this, on his spaceship island with his non-human companion entities...? (and it should be added that years later when I did DMT and found myself walking, at the end, through a windowless version of the Black Swan, the whole experience had been one of encountering non-human inorganic entities, and the windowless hotel was simply the last manifestation of their domain that I "saw").

In the preface to *Difference and Repetition* Deleuze says "A book of philosophy should in part be a very particular species of detective novel, in part a kind of science fiction.[16]" And to this it should be added that, from the very beginning within western philosophy the blocked science-fiction mode of engagement has been a process of fending-off wider and deeper spheres of reality. The two sides of what suppress and cripple human beings are religion, and a fixation on the use of reason, as opposed to lucidity. And one expression of reason-fixation – along with its ordinary, deadening micro-functionings – are the science fiction dead-dreamings of figures such as Plato ("yes, there's something more to reality, and it's the same as mathematics").

In relation to the blocking-system of "reason-revelation" modernism is a spectacular movement of escape. An achieved modernist dreaming, by virtue of it being a dreaming, is at a higher level of abstraction than are the products of reason (because the abstraction here is an expression of both lucidity and reason). But it is important to remember that as twentieth-century modernism progresses and is pushed further toward blocked science-fiction – away from the ancient wilderness and the body without organs – the science fiction that comes more to the forefront is still a world of dreamings. Even the most attenuated of these abstract-oneiric worlds is likely to have a line of flight running through it, no matter how fugitive, or implicit.

But the best dreamings of science fiction are of course utterly modernist. What is the planet Solaris if not both an ancient wilderness and a body without organs? And Sapphire and Steel inhabit a series of worlds which are all wild, "wilderness" spaces with no-one much around – even if they are all buildings at the same time – and are specialists in relation to entities and dimensions which definitely appear to be solely energy-and-intent formations (bodies without organs). Science fiction taken to its own line of flight, crosses over a threshold and becomes something new.

And the oneiric experiences that were heightened – to the point of me focusing on them, and thinking about them – by being at the Black Swan seem to have been "sci-fi living" in a form that was not about fending off what was around me.

* * *

Two days from the end of those ten days at the Black Swan, there was around eight inches of snow over the space of twenty four hours – a blizzard of snow, followed by another blizzard of light. I was now at last encountering at full intensity something that all along I had *felt* as something extraordinary – a kind of pervasive wind-revealing (and terrain-brightening) "action" on the part of the planet.

* * *

Later, during – and after – another long stay at the hotel (perhaps in May) I had the beginnings of a relationship with an 18 year-old girl from London who was working at the hotel (our encounters were kept going through the next hotel being only ten miles away, so that I was able to travel by bus to meet her). This was by far the nearest to a relationship that I reached, during all that year of hotel-nomadism.

I remember that at one point she was talking enthusiastically about an apparently well-known venue in London where punk bands played, and she mentioned a band she really liked and who she expected me to know (almost certainly it was The Clash).

I remember feeling ashamed that I did not know the band, and ashamed that I pretended that I *did* know them.

* * *

The song that blew me away, more than any other, during that summer, was not a song with any influence from punk. It was sung by a woman called Annie Haslam: it was called Northern Lights, and the band was called Renaissance. It *still* seems to me that this is the most sublimely beautiful song from the 1970s.

And somehow the song seems to be about a line of flight toward Love-and-Freedom (to the ultra-intense Love beyond and including relationship-love) which is falling back, collapsing – as well as about the relationship-love that remains at the end of the song:

Destination outward bound
I turn to see the northern lights behind the wing
Horizons seem to beckon me
Learned how to cry too young, so now I live to sing

It's not for money and it's not for fame
I just can't explain, sometimes it's lonely
[...]

I hear your voice, it comforts me
In morning dreams I take your hand, you walk with me
[...]

Destination homeward now
Take the easy way, bring me down
Making the hard way now I see
Hard to be really free, I'm missing you near me.

The northern lights are in my mind
They guide me back to you.

The northern lights are both planetary and human; they are the aurora borealis, and they are a view of Manchester or Leeds at night. And the horizons that seem to beckon are the bright-transcendental, the view of which is under threat of being collapsed to a perception only of home, sex and a relationship.

This song, as sung by Annie Haslam, would be a necessary second starting-point for understanding the eerie within human existence.

9

What might Sapphire and Steel say about the extraordinary beauty and general disastrousness of human existence? If you were a detective looking for what is really happening – all along – in the eerie human hotel, what ideas might come to you?

A first idea might be that, working on the assumption that religions are progressively blocking the escape routes for human beings, we need to work out what has been systematically blocked over the last few thousand years from being a doorway to the body without organs, the "sacred", the transcendental.

The answer here is: *the Planet; Women.*

And it is important to hold in mind that the planet, as a being which creates new beings out of itself, is Spinozistically to be understood as female, so that these two doorways are inter-related (Ariadne's thread is Ariadne...). It is also vital to see that animals are also beings created within the planet, and that these other elements of the planet have also been repressed as doorways to the shamanic Sacred, the body without organs.

The second idea might be that – given the affect of the eerie is indeterminately beautiful and sinister – we have to perceive that the two fundamentally eerie aspects of human existence are *sexuality* and *stories*. It needs to be added to this that sexuality must be taken as inseparable from the state of being *in love*, as well as being the state of erotic arousal, and that stories – or dreamings – here are the worlds of magical, ultra-abstract oneiric tales, and are the stories of religions (also the stories of history and science).

The third idea might be that we have arrived at adulthood pre-stalked, twice over, but with a secret option. We have been pre-stalked from birth by a passive, reproductive fixation (something not at all part of own will), and then as young children we have been successfully stalked by the control mind;

and we all have the secret option to escape across thresholds of awareness toward love, freedom and wider realities.

10

After that first visit to the Black Swan we went to York, and stayed for a week at a hotel called The Chase. About four hundred yards further along the same road was a hotel belonging to a chain of newly built hotels called "post houses" - the York Post House. Both of these hotels were on a long street overlooking York's racecourse. I think we may have stayed at the Post House for a day or so and then continued "next door" for a week at The Chase. Half-way through that week it snowed very heavily, and I heard that all roads into Helmsley were blocked by snow – I remember feeling shut out of the place where I really wanted to be.

Those hotels were on the outskirts of York, around a mile and a half beyond the medieval city wall. We also stayed two or three times at two hotels in the centre, one of them a modern hotel that was alongside the river.

It seems it is necessary to circle across space (and actions) in a way that consists of a vortex, or an upward spiral – to make all of your re-visitings into events in an intensificatory process, rather than repetitions being deadening expressions of habit or compulsion. The "circlings" of my mother's hotel nomadism (with the recurring visits to Northumberland, the Lake District, and Pembrokeshire, as well as the journeys all around the north and west of Yorkshire) were expressions of a lonely and anguished compulsion mixed together with the joy of travelling: they were not an upward spiral at all, but they were a *gap* in ordinary existence. And a gap is a place through which worlds arrive. Looking back on it, I now feel that York for me became a kind of unnoticed dreamer's battleground in a process of awakening (and it seems that a year later in York, in midwinter, I achieved a kind of libidinal-oneiric victory, though one which, for all its fundamental positivity, was also threaded with something dark).

One night in the middle of summer (it was probably June, or July) at the York Post House I had a seismically horrific nightmare. A nightmare that was utter horror, and in a way where there was only feeling – terror – involved, without any images at all, even the moment after I woke up from it. All I was left with was two ways of talking about the horror, both of which came to me in the hours afterwards.

The first way of expressing what had happened in the dream was that it felt as if I had been irreparably and ultra-sadistically separated out across a floor into all of my organs: so that my eyes, heart, brain, skin, lungs – all of my organs – had been spread out across twenty feet of floor, and the fact that I was still alive and feeling and in permanent, day-after-day ultimate torture was being gloated over by a psychotic "evil scientist" figure.

The second way of talking about the horror in the dream was that it had felt as if I had realised that I was falling at great speed a light-years distance through a sky, and that I had fallen onto an infinitely thin needle light-years high which had pierced my heart, and which as I fell onto it was very slowly getting wider, so that I was alive, but with the needle onto which I was falling all the time growing wider by a tiny amount so that eventually but inevitably – maybe years later – it would kill me.

When I woke up from the dream, I was dreaming that in some sense I was fighting something in a life and death struggle, and that I had picked up the three foot wide heavy coffee table in the bedroom to attack what I was defending myself from. I opened my eyes and found that I was on my back in bed actually holding the coffee table – which I was using as a weapon in the dream – and that one of its legs had ripped a foot long hole in one of the sheets of the bed.

Nothing remotely like this had ever happened before, and nothing remotely like it has ever happened since. Understandably I was more than a little shocked by this oneiric earthquake. But I pulled myself together immediately that morning, and of course, with no recurrence, it was possible to forget about it – write it off as an anomaly – and move on.

The only preceding event to which I connect this experience – and I have always made this connection – is the fact that over the previous few days I had read the "black humour" satirical novel *Wilt*, by Tom Sharpe. I remember that this novel left me with the sense that I had been reading something bleakly unpleasant: as if the novel had an integrity in pointing out things about sex and violence and power (power has a wide sense here: I was struck by a scene where there is a party at which people are drinking while watching the Watergate footage of Nixon's meltdown interviews during or prior to his impeachment), but where the integrity is all along in the service of something concupiscent and laughingly malicious. Wilt – a teacher at a polytechnic who decides to do a trial "murder" of his wife using an inflatable doll and a building-site excavation – was simply a bleak object of supposedly satirical or farcical horror, but I remember feeling a kind of dismay at becoming aroused by the extra-marital sexual encounters of Wilt and his wife. As if I had been drawn into the libidinal field of something far more twisted than it was pretending to be.

A first question is: if humour is all along the third form of outer-edge abstraction alongside fiction and philosophy (and it is possibly the most powerful of the three) then do we need to pay more attention to the libidinal, oneiric-metaphysical philoso-phies we are absorbing all along through the works of our satirists, comedians and everyday "humourists"?

And the second question is: looking back on the vortex of my experiences during 1978, what exactly was the struggle taking place at the centre of this eerie storm?

11

Thinking now about the first half of 1978, and the end of 1977 (my hotel-nomad life began in October 1977) I am left with the impression that I was like a rabbit who manages to get a paw into a snare just before it tightens. But the impression is that I was simply lucky enough to gain a potentially life-saving advantage as the trap closed, not at all that this happened through skill.

The detail of this impression has an eerie quality of being multiply determined. Many years later, under strikingly intense circumstances, I found a rabbit caught in a snare, with one paw in the wire saving it from asphyxiation – but not from death – and I dug out the stake to which the snare was attached and saved it (you don't escape on your own).

It is also the case that in November of 1977 I read – and was profoundly affected by – Richard Adams' novel *Watership Down*.

Watership Down is very definitely a modernist novel. Its epigrams at the start of the chapters, and its whole trajectory, place everything in a zone of indiscernibility between Britain and the classical Greek/Roman world (the opening epigram is from Aeschylus's *Agamemnon*, and at a crucial point a few chapters later there is a reference to the Odyssey). The change of perspective transforms all of England into an enigmatically dangerous arcadia (by different means this is the same kind of result achieved by the ur-modernist Shakespeare with the forest in *A Midsummer Night's Dream*). And the body without organs – with its complete fluidity concerning contact "at a distance" - is evinced by the divinatory dreams of its recurrently agonised shaman figure, Fiver (the connection with shamanism is explicit – one of the epigrams quotes a book about the "spirit journeys" of shamanism).

It is also a novel with an exceptionally eerie episode at its "centre". The visit to the death-cult warren, where the rabbits' poetry melancholically celebrates death (they are being given food by a farmer who is killing them), and where the rabbits display an "unnatural gentleness," is one of the most eerie events imaginable.

I bought the book in the small bookshop in Malton, in early November (I don't remember making any connection at the time, but one of the chapter titles for the events at the death-cult warren is "like trees in November"). A sixth intent-current was now making itself felt, although it had been strongly in effect all along, through circumstances in my life, and through earlier dreamings that had swept me away. This is the intent-current of animals – of animals perceived shamanically as fellow beings on the planet who are on exactly the same level as humans.

This intent-current has in fact been very intensely (though obliquely) in effect within English modernism since natural history created a metaphysical rupture at Oxford in the early 1860s (leaving in its wake the surrealism of "who do we take seriously, bishops or dinosaurs?"), and since Lewis Carroll gave expression to part of what had broken free by creating a world in which animals are fully alongside human beings. The oneiric emergence is then taken further in a first phase by writers such as Kenneth Graeme (the numinous power of "The Piper at the Gates of Dawn" has been pointed out, and has been artistically invoked, but has not been generally recognised) and Dunsany, with the foxes in *The King of Elfland's Daughter*. But the highest point of this obscured tradition in 1977 was probably *Watership Down*, whose author had been inspired in part by a natural history book, *The Private Life of the Rabbit* (1964), and whose final epigram is from Carroll, referring to the rabbit protagonist Hazel – "He was part of my dream, of course – but then I was part of his dream, too."

12

Many years later (in 2007): I am asleep in my tent in an area of forested, mountain wilderness in the northwest of Patagonia. Every day of the previous 10 weeks in Patagonia I had written a very short story (perhaps they averaged 600 words) alternating every day between the viewpoints of a specific man (a created character, not myself), a specific woman, and a cat.

I dreamed I was in a long-abandoned soviet base somewhere deep in Siberian forest. I had the clear knowledge at the very start of the dream that the place was very far from any human habitation (I felt this as an exceptionally positive thing, and there was a phrase in my mind like "two days walk from anywhere in any direction"). The first view of the base was from the outside, from a track arriving from the west. It was daylight, in summer. After that I was in an area inside it, which had some smallish buildings on one side, including an attached fifty foot high wooden tower, which I knew in the dream had been used over the years of dereliction by people observing birds. Fifty feet diagonally opposite these buildings across an area of grass there is a line of things that I think could be small missile silos (although in the dream the feeling of the original purpose of the base is indeterminate between military and space-exploration). Behind them is thick forest, and alongside on the right, and immediately opposite the buildings, there is a wall of encroaching trees.

I found myself at the top of the observation tower, a rectangular space with a wooden floor. Looking at objects left on this floor (maybe a box of matches is one of them) the idea arrives in the dream that there are people living on the base.

At some point in the dream (I could never place the event in the sequence of the other occurrences) I go over to the wall of trees. And animals of different kinds start coming along branches of the trees toward me – tree-animals, perhaps like racoons, also a lynx-sized cat... It is a moment of profoundly moving depth-level communication. I am being greeted and welcomed, and at the same time I am greeting and welcoming them. I am intensely grateful for their opening up of contact, given all that has happened between humans and other animals – and I am welcoming them to myself. Everything is at the level of feeling and intent – we communicate by sharing our states of being.

In a part of the dream that apparently in some sense continues from my being on the top of the tower, I am suddenly aware that I am floating in mid-air in a room at ground level below the tower, and that I am being shown how to literally be beyond gravity by three very beautiful women who are also in mid-air in the room, and who are part of a small group of people who are living in the base during the summer.

A moment later I am with two men, in another room, alongside the first one. At the very beginning of this part of the dream the men tell me that the women are not here now, when I am in a more-awake state, because when women with whom I could fall in love are present, my choices are continually inflected by sexual desire. They point out this fact to me as something that I need to change.

The two men are sitting on the far side of a table. One of them reads an astonishingly brilliant, abstract-oneiric prose poetry passage from a book he is holding. I ask to hear something again, that I have not quite grasped. When the man responds he reads out something completely different, but equally brilliant. I insist on seeing the book, and discover that what I am reading is also astonishing, but that the passage is different again from either of the passages that the man "read out". The friendly laughter of the men makes me aware that I am being shown the direction of spontaneity and lucid improvisation, and that I am being told that I am neurotic.

At the end of the dream I am suddenly outside a train station in London – very familiar to me from commuting – and I am distressed because I have accidentally got my girlfriend pregnant at a time when an escape is taking place on the part of a group of friends, with the pregnancy understood by me as something that would be deleterious to the group escape.

And then suddenly- and this is the very end of the dream – I am stroking a female cat that is looking at me as I stroke it, and that is reaching sexual ecstasy. As the cat reaches orgasm – it vanishes.

I wake up, in the tent, in Patagonia.

* * *

Why the feeling that in the months before the second half of 1978 something valuable was arriving, an advantage that heightened my chances of surviving a trap that was closing around me?

A first basis for the feeling is maybe that I had reached, through *Watership Down*, a vantage on the world that saw dreams as *perceptions* of aspects of the world (however muddled and blurred this perception might generally be) - and at their most extraordinary, as sustained views of the outside of ordinary reality. Richard Adams's midsummer dreaming had done its modernist work and taken me back 3000 years to the semi-shamanic world of Homeric Greece, a time when everyone knew that dreams recurrently are glimpses toward the Outside. This vantage was then strengthened by my reading *The Shining*, another book whose dreams do not fit at all with the deadly, blocking modality of modernism's shadow, psychoanalysis. As Bob Dylan says, in 1965 –

At dawn my lover comes to me
And tells me of her dreams
With no attempt to shovel the glimpse
Into the ditch of what each one means [17]

A second basis is maybe the eerie dream about the people living in the Andes thousands of years ago – the dream that took place at the Talbot Hotel in the spring of 1978. I did a drawing of this dream the next day, and then I gave no further thought to it. But it was a dream that I nonetheless kept remembering, and which became central to my memories of the Talbot.

The third source of the impression is the fact that during that time I fell in love with *a place*. I fell in love with the area around and between Malton and Helmsley. I had found a place which was a gap through which bright, heightening affects and dreamings arrived: an inside of my circlings and wanderings that was worth having as a centre only because it was really the outside. Under different circumstances – subtracting the nomadism – I would almost certainly have settled down there in a relationship, and the centre would have stopped being the outside, becoming simply another territory.

* * *

(It is as if the Place that had been found had a highest-energy, highest-lucidity "centre" in the form of Malton – furthest south, out on a limb extending into the outside – and an internal, maximally secluded and heartening "centre" in the form of Helmsley. The area is "Ryedale" – going upstream the Rye is the river that "runs" from the Derwent through Helmsley and into the maze of wooded hills beyond it, and is a part of the river-system of the streams that run down from all of the hidden dales. But the name is here being used for the "horseshoe" of hills consisting of the western moorland of the North York Moors, the Hambleton Hills west of Helmsley, and the Howardian Hills that run down to where the Derwent meanders its way through a valley a few miles west of Malton).

* * *

1978 was the year when *Watership Down* was turned into an animated film. The film is far from a failure, but it is only partially in contact with what is most valuable about the book.

The strengths of *Watership Down* are its modernism by means of a becoming-animal, its view of dreaming as a disguised form of perception and abstract-perception, and the way in which an aspect of its dangerous arcadia suggests the human household has a melancholy death-cult at work within it, and is suffused with the "eerie laughter" [18] of capitulation to power, to deadly domination. It is thought-provoking that, despite having had very little kudos (it was initially sold as a book for children), it has sold more copies than any other Penguin novel. The great joy and value of becomings has been at work in this, the joy of becomings which is at such a height that it is invisible – no-one notices that their friend or child has become a rabbit.

Perhaps the only way in which the book is directed a little toward children is that it softens the blow for those waking up in the direction of a shamanic perception of dreaming (but of course most "adult" books in this respect are child's bedtime stories to a far greater extent). Fiver, the seer, is only confronted with disbelief and annoyance. Whereas the capitalist world's conjoined rationalism and religion confront with responses that range right across the continuum from the diagnosis of schizophrenia, through ridicule (now the most common response) to accusations of heresy and of evil contact with spirits.

* * *

But it should be asked – what about women in this world? And also, what about the trap – the snare – in which I was caught in 1978?

Watership Down has no central female characters at all, and the very peripheral female characters it does have are stereotyped nurturing figures. And it is in 1977 that Ursula Le Guin, in the middle of writing *The Eye of the Heron*, realises that she has been writing sci-fi books as an "honorary man", and does not know how to write about women. As Deleuze and Guattari point out at around this time, becoming-woman is fundamental, not just for men, but also for women.

(I do not want to give a distorted impression of Le Guin – there is surely no greater writer of fantasy/science-fiction novels).

But what shadows and spectres are lurking as men set out on this very obscured path? The Cheshire cat's smiling ability to disappear takes it out of the reach of dark instances of power, but for a young male such fluency with avoidance of attacks – whether from "within" or from the social world – are likely to be a long way in the future.

13

If it had begun with four men dreaming of women, by 1978 it was primarily a world of women. Even in bands where the songwriters were men, the singing was being done by women. The Beatles had been central to the beginning, but now, at its deepest level pop-rock pre-eminently consisted of women dreaming of the Outside – and dreaming of some relationship with men that would not be damaging to them.

In that year and the previous four:

Stevie Nicks: Rhiannon
Patti Smith: Horses
Donna Summer: I Feel Love
Joni Mitchell: Hejira
Agnetha Faltskog, Anni-frid Lyngstad: Dancing Queen
Kate Bush: Wuthering Heights
Annie Haslam: Northern Lights

And so the question is: what is the relationship of women to the eerie arcadia of modernism?

It seems that something was left behind at Delphi. Women have a facility for lucidity, and it was a woman who was always "the oracle" who spoke at Delphi (apparently riddling words are one form in which lucidity can be expressed). And all of the indications are that Delphi was originally the centre of a planet-focused and cosmos-focused "mother goddess" shamanism (a stone at Delphi was called the "omphalos", which means "navel"). A shamanism which was able to see both the planet and women as windows toward the bright-transcendental – toward the Love-and-Freedom within the body without organs. It was this that was suppressed by the imposition of the Apollo cult onto

Delphi, with the male priest who would now "interpret" the words of the oracle.

At around the same time as the destruction of the earlier Delphi tradition the Homeric stories are in many ways a brutal attack on women. They are denuded magical tales of a war-obsessed culture, where the gods have become formulaic forces of assistance for warrior heroes (like characters in a bad graphic novel), presided over by a male god, Zeus. In the world of Odysseus the two primary roles for the female are that of dark, seducing enchantress (the witch Circe is echoed in *The Odyssey* by the sirens) and ultimate, domestic-goddess home-maker (Penelope).

It is into this damaged oneiric space that Plato arrives, with his reason-cult. And the spectacle is of Sophocles alongside him, trying to dream his way back to the abandoned outlands of his people, where in glades in mountain forests there is powerful, beautiful music, and where anomalous female and male beings will teach you that dance is the fundamental direction for waking lucidity.

* * *

Within the eerie arcadia of modernism is a becoming-woman, a becoming lucid. A dancing brightness and abandon – "you've got to lose control" - and an ability to reach "the eye of the forest" (both these quotation are from Patti Smith's *Horses*), the place from which it is possible to see the true nature of the world. In 1978 the sheer joy and beauty of this eerie arcadia has been trying to wake for some years (1975 was the high-point) and it was perhaps inevitable that women's' voices would come to the forefront.

* * *

The following writing is an "abstract-story" that was originally an email that I sent to three friends in December of 2012:

To understand love is to embody the understanding, to live it.

When a man starts to love a woman with all of his being he is setting out on a momentous journey. To love someone is to see and feel the world from their perspective, from their world of intent and embodiment. How otherwise could he truly dance with her? (love is a dance of becomings). But for the man, attaining this new dreaming – or experience – of embodiment turns out to be an immense transformation – one that shatters his idea of himself, and his idea of the world.

For the man, to dream the perspective of the woman he loves is to experience her love and her lucidity, the world of her intent, feeling and awareness. But it is also both to experience her desire – causing him to live the bliss of feminine sexual abandon while in the state of being in love – and to experience sexuality in a focused way (now drawing on both male and female perspectives) as partly the working of a will that is not our own in the very centre of what we are accustomed to see as our own libidinal intent. Experiencing the bliss of in-love feminine sexual abandon causes a man to wonder about his sexuality, not initially realising that in fact there is nothing more male than to do this. But seeing sexuality as in part the working of a will that is not our own is in many ways an even more shattering discovery.

The second discovery becomes two-fold. It becomes clear that human beings have been set up, by a transcendental force, to be reproducers (to be encased, immense – but unfocused – worlds of awareness that produce more worlds of awareness of the same kind), and that they have been simultaneously given the chance to break free toward love and freedom and wider realities. This second option is the chance to metamorphose into the being who you really are.

It becomes clear to the man at this point that the incredible brightness of women is all along to do with them having a special ability – the ability to give birth to the future. Women are practitioners of the art of "evolution" (metamorphosis of lives). Men also have this ability, but they only have it at a lower level.

When a woman starts to love a man with all of her being she is in immense danger. She is crossing an abyss not so much of sexual self-questioning, but of danger of abandonment toward domination, toward "sweet" (in fact increasingly hideous) socially enshrined enslavement. BUT – if lucidity is starting to wake between the woman and the man, something extraordinary starts to happen as the woman begins to achieve the dreaming of the perspective of the man's intent and embodiment.

Women have a far greater natural facility for lucidity than men. In becoming the man, the woman wakes her own lucidity, by receiving a boost for this mode of contact with the world. Evidently she also becomes male sexual intent, but the utterly vital transformation is that she wakes her lucidity. Women show their ability all the time for outsights about the deeper and wider nature of the world – outsights toward intent, dreaming, feeling and awareness. But they do not allow this ability to focus itself into a deliberate, focused, sustained attention.

Women – particularly beautiful women – all have immense power to attract and affect the people around them through being women, through having female brightness. And from a very early age an unconscious agreement has been extracted from women that they will never create the – in fact, liberatory – rupture of a sustained, lucid contesting of male metaphysics of rationality (rationality is a lower form of intelligence than lucidity, possessed by women just as much as by men) and of revelation, or religion. This agreement is key to female enslavement by men, because in agreeing to never wake lucidity – to never "commit rupture" - she has in effect agreed to never really start thinking at the level of her true, hidden ability for understanding.

But now the woman looks around her. And she sees that intent and dreaming and feeling and awareness run through every-thing. She sees that intent and feeling and dreaming and awareness are what give rise to "things" ("solid" being) and that intent and feeling suffuse everything, and are what every-thing is at the deepest level. She sees that knowledge most fundamentally is about *embodying* knowledge. She sees that sexuality in part, before metamorphosis toward love and freedom, is the working of a deleterious intent that is not our own (she sees that calling it nature is simply a failure to think, and that calling it god's will is a male scam producing the metaphysical domination of women ("I'm being fucked by a man, and I'm also being fucked by the will of god")).

She sees that maps for journeying forward into the world (whether in the form of magical tales, collections of sayings, or descriptions) are only of value if they are outsights that guide you toward travelling into the unknown, in the direction of love and freedom (descriptions that claim to provide an account of some ultimate, transcendent unknown-which-is-now-revealed become visible as impositions – as invalid, and deleterious overall in their effects).

She sees that we have to become the Love, Freedom and Lucidity that, all along, we are.

* * *

My own eerie experiences in the second half of 1978 took place away from the valleys and the hilly, wooded vale-country with which I had fallen in love. They took place down on "the plain", and right alongside the rivers of this plain (the Vale of York, as opposed to the Vale of Pickering).

At some time in July or August I was staying in a bleak, modern hotel on the edge of a small town called Wetherby (twenty miles to the northwest of York). It was by a roundabout leading onto the A1, and was alongside the River Wharfe.

One night, in my room at the hotel, I reached a new level of ultra-erotic intensity. I fantasised that I was being seduced by a woman who was working in a department store. The mode of seduction of the woman was to convince me that it was now normal and right – for men in general – to wear women's' sensual, erotic clothing, and was to move from initially recommending less alluring "magical objects", to recommending garments that were maximally feminine/sexual.

I was blown away by the level of sexual bliss that I reached in the course of this virtual-real seduction.

But of course afterwards – yearning to get back to that level of bliss – I had been jolted sideways from any idea that my life made sense in relation to love and desire. I longed to have a love relationship with a woman. But I could not imagine that the strong and intensely feminine women to whom I was attracted would have any libidinal interest in the new aspect of the line of flight of becoming-woman that had appeared.

It was indeed a line of flight, a very powerful one, although nonetheless intrinsically it was immensely less powerful than the line of flight of being in love with a woman.

But – blowing completely aside the haze of psychoanalysis for a moment – who was that woman in the department store? The woman who taught me feminine abandon – but an abandon that was a letting go to far too great an extent in the direction of feminine submission to domination (as opposed to the true femininity of lucidly letting go toward Love-and-Freedom). Given that the virtual-real is no less real than the actual-real, what might have been the nature of this "encounter"?

Department stores do not have windows, like the version of the Black Swan Hotel in which I found myself on the occasion when I took DMT. To blow away, in turn, the haze of the thought of such places (but very much not just for that reason) the following piece of writing should be included at this point. It was written in 2008, about a year after the dream that I had when I was in Patagonia.

Toward Tuva

We had been living in the abandoned base for a month. That day I decided to go for a walk on my own in the pine-forested hills that straggled to the south.

The base was thirty miles from anywhere, deep in southern taiga forest, not far from the border with Tuva. In some directions, including the one I was walking towards, it was a hundred miles from anywhere. All of which is to say that it was somewhere to a much greater extent than most places.

I found myself in a ragged glade on the summit of a flat-topped hill that seemed to be vast in extent, a kind of taiga massif, a pine-covered escarpment plateau. In the distance beyond some trees I could see the conical shape of a grassy outcrop. As I walked toward the trees I discovered that an animal was coming toward me along a dead branch of a Siberian pine. The animal made me think of an opossum, it looked at me with wide, striking eyes. I had an odd feeling, both that this was its place, and always had been, and that it was somehow not averse to meeting me there. There was a warmth and lucidity in its eyes that startled me, and made me feel like an outsider fortunate to be welcomed.

Then the animal was gone. It whisked back along the branch, and disappeared into the forest. As I tried to follow it with my eyes, I had a feeling I had seen another animal, much larger, the size of a lynx, off to the left of where I was looking.

I climbed the outcrop feeling a strange euphoria, an obscure sense of a comradeship with the animals of that place. At the top I could see a straggle of low mountains to the south. I had a sudden flash, where the knoll on which I was standing was made of a kind of dark, solid air, into which I could see. It was faintly spiroid in form, and internally flanged with curved, deep-violet planes, and near-immobile vortical energy-forms, and I felt it as just the tip of a bright darkness of intent.

I walked the ten miles back to the base. It had been the year before that myself and Tanya and Alan had discovered the derelict terrain of buildings – apparently abandoned in the 1950s. Its purpose was unknown, although it was clearly military in some sense. This time Teresa and Sergei were here as well. The five of us had been encamped there for all of July, having the party of our lives, although it could also be described as something much better, and more focused than a party.

When I slept that night I dreamed there were other people

living in the base. They had been there for months. Their rooms were in a building that did not exist in actuality, a ramshackle building with a kind of viewing tower on one side. In the dream I suddenly found myself with them, two women, and two men, all four of them utterly different from each other, but each in their own way with a striking quality of sparkling humour, and intense, uncanny resourcefulness.

A moment later I discovered I was in a city that seemed to be somewhere in south or central America. Everywhere the buildings clearly belonged to an ancient forgotten struggle, they were warrior, military buildings belonging to a conflict lost to memory thousands of years before. Everyone was encamped in the buildings but they knew nothing about their original purpose.

Then I was in a city that somehow I knew to be London. The buildings were the same. They again belonged to a long-forgotten desperate conflict. People were inhabiting these buildings – they had converted them in endless ways – but again, they were living in military buildings belonging to a war that no-one remembered. I knew the reason no-one knew about this struggle. It was because human beings had been defeated, and the forgetting was a result of the defeat.

For a moment I was drifting above ground level alongside a dried-up lake that seemed to be on a run-down estate somewhere in England. There were people around, and there was a striking, focused feeling of joy and exhilaration.

Then I was back in the base, walking out of a room where I had been in mid-air, and where the two women had been telling me that in some fundamental sense gravity is a state of mind.

In the second room the two men told me things – laughingly they told me to abandon self-importance and self-indulgence. And it was clear that primarily by self-indulgence they meant allowing sexual desire for women to do "the thinking" in my life.

I woke up with Tanya sleeping alongside me, birds were singing, and the sun was visible through the fabric of the tent.

14

In late September of 1984 I was on my own in a house to the east of Malton, and was edgy with frustration, waiting to get away, in a week's time, to begin studying at the adult education college in North Wales – Coleg Harlech. Unable to cope with the inaction I set out one afternoon to cycle to the moors, taking almost no food with me, and no tent or sleeping bag (I didn't own these pieces of equipment), and believing that I would stay for two or three nights in the moors, sleeping in woods. I cycled on tiny lanes across the Rye valley in the direction of Farndale, arriving at Kirkbymoorside in the early evening, and then continuing onto the long slope of hill-land that rises toward the villages of Gillamoor and Fadmoor. It started to get dark and cold – and feeling despondent and foolish, I turned round, and cycled all the way back, getting home at some time around midnight.

(To get a better understanding of what is meant by an intent-current, I will point out that the intent-current of the planet – after having been insistently in effect in the background – only went at last into full effect when I set out on my own to walk across the Pyrenees, about eleven years ago, in 2003 (there had been failed "attempts" when I had gone into wildernesses, but under the wrong circumstances). On this trip I found my way into a compellingly beautiful area of mountains (one for which I had no map) that I walked through for several days. Being in this unknown and wonderful terrain jolted me free – in a whole series of ways – from locked-down forms of perception, thought and action).

There are "illusions" in human existence which are really vital views of the way to the Outside, only we misinterpret them and are left with a perturbed longing – stemming from confusion about nearness to the goal, and a lack of lucid, fluid subtlety in our approach. During times in the past when I was not in a relationship I noticed that in my yearning state I was prone to the feeling, on seeing or meeting a woman to whom I was attracted, that if we started a relationship *everything* would be alright – everything would instantly be taken over a threshold into lucidity and the absence of subjectified, reactive emotions.

And looking back over my experiences in the late 70s and early 80s I am aware of a striking tendency I had, under certain circumstances, to feel that if I was to just walk off permanently into some area of beautiful countryside, everything would work out well, even without any money, and if I wanted I would be able to find a life there.

* * *

The first walk I remember in the area around Malton and Helmsley must have been in March or April of 1978. I set off early, at around 8.30, from the Talbot Hotel, and I was rapidly in the hills that stretch west by northwest in a broad expanse that ends eighteen miles away in a terrain of slightly lower hills, and in one idyllic, very narrow, hill-ridge, where the road dips and rises in at least two switchbacks of the grassy, field-covered ridge. Rising beyond these hills are the North York Moors.

I remember walking alongside the wall of a large estate, and that afterwards someone to whom I spoke at the hotel was surprised that I had not been aware that I was walking alongside the grounds of Castle Howard (a sign saying "Castle Howard" would have meant nothing to me), but my aim had been *to get into the hills*, and the idea of gigantic houses and estates of the English aristocracy would have been inimical to what I was dreaming about. Two years before, Kubrick had been at Castle Howard, filming Barry Lyndon, but even if I had known about Kubrick this would not have impacted on what I was doing. I was trying to leave behind the human world in all its "urbane" aspects, and reach the most remote, atmospheric area of countryside I could find (I was trying to reach the planet).

I also once cycled from Thornton le Dale – a village east of Pickering – to an area of hill-land to the south of Rosedale that was an expanse of silver birch and bracken and small woods and fields. I found a place where you could look west at a series of seven or eight, glacier-carved buttress escarpments which extended all the way to the far, western end of the moors, beyond Bransdale. I found this view very impressive (I knew these hills were a singular aspect of the terrain), and I was also set dreaming by the area of heathland and silver birch trees. It was somewhere that made stories appear effortlessly in your mind. I think a story started from the idea that it was the kind of place where a band might go to write the songs for an album, but this detail does not do enough to suggest the dream-inspiring atmosphere. I was reaching the Future, the way you do as a child (when a child goes into a semi-wild or derelict place they effortlessly dream up virtual-real worlds).

I had found a Place (or it had found me). But a Place in this sense is not a personal, subjective thing. Other people will have been aware of it. Looking down from the perspective of the planet on the area around Malton and Helmsley it is important to look at what has been happening in the thousand years since the goddesses were swept away. There is Castle Howard, and three other large stately homes, there are the ruins of two monasteries (Rievaulx and Byland), there is the Catholic public school Ampleforth College, and there are four ruined Norman castles (all nine of these are in an area which is only around fifteen miles across).

But for now these facts should just be taken as indicators of the striking beauty of this terrain – Ryedale and the moors and wooded hills that surround it. Slip sideways from the gravity of the socio-religious domain, and stand on some south-facing part of that heathland on the edge of the moors, and see for a moment what is blocked by whatever is dark and deleterious within human sexuality, human dogmatic stories, and human control-behaviour. The planet – the escape-multiplicities of Love-and-Freedom: the serene lightning and dance of the becomings.

(The child, in being swept into dreams, is on the threshold of lucidity).

15

At the Black Swan, in the summer of 1978, I read *Imperial Earth*, having found it in a rotating stand of books by the hotel's reception desk. Maybe two months before the same thing had happened with *The Shining* at The Talbot.

Three years afterwards – during one of the later phases of hotel nomadism, after a long gap, during which I had spent a year working in a grocery shop, in a village near Malton – I was at the Black Swan again, and I read *Wuthering Heights*. I had found a hard-back copy (perhaps forty years old) in one of the hotel's ancient lounge rooms, the one with the leaded windows, with flawed, diamond-shaped panes of glass. As a child I had read and enjoyed *Jane Eyre*, but I had stopped reading Emily Bronte's novel after the first twenty pages.

Wuthering Heights and *Imperial Earth*. Taste these two titles, and feel how different they are. And the two novels themselves could barely be more different.

However, between them they form a starting point for thinking about the eerie in the human world – and not simply through contrast. In both novels there are two men who are in love with the same woman, and the woman in both cases is called Catherine. The two women are also both known by a "diminutivised" name. In Emily Bronte's novel the shortened form of the name is Cathy, in Arthur C. Clarke's it is Calindy (shortened from Catherine Linden Ellerman). It is also perhaps relevant to mention that *Imperial Earth* starts with the sound of the wind – only this is the wind on the surface of Titan, the world (the largest moon of Saturn) on which both of the male characters live. In *Imperial Earth* both male characters – the protagonist Duncan, and his friend Karl – are scientists, although Duncan is primarily an administrator and engineer. If there is a Heathcliff figure in the novel it is Karl, who is wildly "reckless" in his relationship with

Calindy, to the point of inflicting damage upon himself: he is also a slightly aloof scientific "genius".

The original sub-title of *Imperial Earth* was "A Fantasy of Love and Discord" (dropped after the initial edition), and the scrapping of this attempt to foreground love in relation to the novel seems to fit with the epigram "every man has business and desire", and with the whole novel in terms of its ostensible focus. There is no doubt that the state of being *in love* finds expression in *Wuthering Heights* (although evidently there are problems with the macho "passionateness" of Heathcliff), and there is also no doubt that a love for the planet finds expression in Emily Bronte's book (Cathy dreams that she is in heaven pleading with the angels to be allowed to return to the moors). But in *Imperial Earth*, even though the novel is all about a journey to Earth from Titan, and about the love on the part of two men for Calindy, the novel shows a noticeable lack of love for the planet and an equally noticeable lack of love for women.

* * *

It is primarily through patriotism that people draw a sense of being "special" from the planet. They do this through the mediating zone of the human world – the part, that is, of the human world which is their territory. In this way they feel that they are special, that their part of the world is special (it is a "sacred" region of the earth in some sense) and that so is their society. In this way people draw energy – inspiration, encouragement, joy – from the planet, while simultaneously despising it as really a part of blind, brute nature. This mediation that prevents sustained deliberate contact almost always involves – to some degree – a secondary blocking-system in the form of a religion (attention is drawn even further away – "yes, there is the sacred, but it is the Gods, or God; or divine consciousness, Buddha consciousness" etc).

But alongside this (in the systems of the control mind) there is the species patriotism of the reason cult. With this mode of mediated contact people draw energy by means of the idea of belonging to the "special-consciousness" world of the human spirit, with its products in the form of reason, knowledge, technologies, and systems of classification. Contact with the world in which we live – the planet – is here mediated and blocked by micro-processes of relating elements to accounts, theories and classifications, with all of these being understood as wondrous features of "man" which are separate from nature... (*Imperial Earth* inhabits this second form of patriotism, but it is not without elements of the first – it is all about a visit to Earth for a celebration of the anniversary of American independence).

Exactly the same situation applies with women. Immense, fundamental energy is drawn from women in a way that is intrinsically connected to them being seen as delightful, beautiful, warm, wonderful. But simultaneously they are demeaned as frivolous, inferior, closer to nature (which is conceived as separate from humans and inferior), prone to engage with superficialities, incapable of sustained abstract thought, secondary. Here the religions function, again, as additional blocking systems (religions come into focus as secondary adjuncts, all along, to the processes of control-mind extraction of energy from women and the planet). After an initial need for plausibility the religions slowly, across millennia, strip away all goddesses from their systems (this process is ongoing within Hinduism, but has already gone a very long way even here) and generally find ways of explicitly or implicitly constructing women as secondary, inferior – as child-rearing subordinates of men.

Women themselves are trapped into this attitude, in relation to other women, by the labyrinth of libidinal constructs of revelation-and-reason (women are closer to nature; their role is to be lovely adjuncts of men, etc) and also by control-mind jealousy which looks at women and sees correctness in the accusations while generally making some kind of personal exemption. From this (dark) point of view what would be the disturbance-power of seeing a lucid, beautiful woman – say a friend who is crossing a threshold of awareness – as being in some sense a window to the Outside, the Future? For jealousy this situation – or anything approaching it – is strictly intolerable.

* * *

But – given that lucidity and brightness and abandon (toward love and freedom, as opposed to power) are aspects of the hidden blocked nature of men, as well as women, then who on earth are men, once you have stripped from them the geekery and gravity of the control mind? Once dominatory "passion-ateness" has been dropped, recognised as a form of disguised violence, and the system of brisk "seriousness," outrage and grave judgementalness (often hidden behind false lightness and irony), has been seen and left behind as yet more imposition and domination, what would a man be like?

These are not empty questions – the philosophy of the eerie in relation to men (who are primary carriers of the control-mind "virus") starts precisely here with the elaboration and answering of these questions. And three extraordinary abstract traditions – separated by thousands of miles and two thousand five hundred years – are all valuable in beginning to answer them.

* * *

The *Tao Te Ching* quietly – and very intensely – does what it can to point out that both men and women need to go in the direction of the female, toward lucidity, fluid improvisation and abandon.

Knowing the masculine
And nurturing the feminine

You become the river of all beneath heaven. [19]

In asking both women and men "Can you be female...?" [20] (are you capable of being female?) the *Tao Te Ching* is asserting that there is something in every sense fundamental about the female or the feminine (it does not ask the same question in relation to maleness). The following passage gives emphasis to this assertion, and again has no maleness equivalent:

> The valley spirit never dies.
> It's called *dark female-enigma*,
> And the gateway of dark female-enigma
> Is called *the root of heaven and earth*,
> Gossamer [...] unceasing [...]
> Use it: it's effortless. [21]

(a question of becoming-woman, but also of entering into becoming with the air, openness, composed, enclosing consistency, and river-flow of a valley).

Florinda Donner's *Being-in-Dreaming* (the subtitle is *An Initiation into the Sorcerers' World*) sets out how men have an inbuilt tendency to try to reason their way toward a lucid awareness, whereas women have a facility (which they have been taught to never use) for seeing the – non-concrete – wider and deeper aspects of the world, or for reaching "the abstract":

> Women are able to open themselves directly to the source, or rather, the source reaches them directly [...] Sorcerers say that women's' connection to knowledge is expansive. On the other hand, men's connection is quite restricted. Men are close to the concrete [...] and aim at the abstract. Women are close to the abstract and yet try to indulge themselves with the concrete.[22]

Men simply have to slip themselves past the "catch" of gravity, "control/imposition" and fixation on the male side of reason (there is also "a female side of reason," as well as lucidity, or the ability to see the abstract): "Sorcerers are able to align themselves to intent [...] because they have given up what specifically defines their masculinity."[23]

And lastly in *A Thousand Plateaus* Deleuze and Guattari are very clear about the primary, fundamental nature of becoming-woman:

"...all becomings begin with and pass through becoming-woman. It is the key to all the other becomings." [24].

* * *

I distantly felt a kind of urbane wrongness about *Imperial Earth* – an elusive but permeating quality of it being both sentimental in its "grandeur" and simultaneously cynical (along with "for every man has business and desire" the second epigram is "remember them and write them off" (in relation to friends/lovers). It had an apparent vastness, but it did not set me dreaming.

It is in fact a product of blocked sci-fi modernism, and modernism denuded to the point where it barely evinces the body without organs at all. Which in part is to say of course that it is the product of the 2500 year old reason-cult (like Pythagoras, Karl is a "genius" with solving geometrical and mathematical problems).

* * *

Wuthering Heights was a jolt of wild, visionary energy. But it left a kind of "grey" aftertaste. There were glimpses toward the Outside in the descriptions of Cathy and Heathcliff before the disaster of Edgar Linton/Thrushcross Grange, but after that almost everything was devastation: and in particular there is the collapse of Heathcliff from the lightness of running wild on the moors with Cathy into the brooding gravity of control-mind maleness. Cathy saying "I *am* Heathcliff!" points toward the fact that being in love always consists of becomings. ("I've dreamt in my life dreams that have stayed with me" says Cathy "[...] and altered the colour of my mind" [25]). But Heathcliff's "I *cannot* live without my soul!" comes at the end of him raging angrily at her in the world of ghosts in which he believes she now exists, and has a quality that is very different from what he does not say - "I *am* Cathy". It fits too well with the grim gender role-assignment of "women are more soulful, men are more forcefully passionate" (meaning men should be excused for their violence), and in the story it seems primarily to function as a justification for Heathcliff's suicide by starvation (a self-immolation which he thinks will take him toward Cathy).

The awareness of – and love for – the planet is the other fundamental strength of the novel, along with the extraordinary awareness of the power of being in love. But it as if the novel falls short at the end not through excessive bleakness, but through not being quite bleak enough (which in part is to say that it is not *eerie* enough, in that the anomalous strangeness of the world of *Wuthering Heights* consists of a romanticised, but conventional dimension of ghosts, or possible ghosts). Although the voice of Lockwood is not that of Emily Bronte, it is his perspective on death and human existence that gives the final note of the story:

> I lingered around them, under that benign sky; watched the moths fluttering among the heath, and harebells; listened to the soft wind breathing through the grass; and wondered how anyone could ever imagine unquiet slumbers for the sleepers in that quiet earth.

The jolt that must be defended here is firstly the thought of human beings going down fighting into a termination of their love and lucidity that will not be a sleep from which they will eventually wake. And secondly it is the question: what forces – psychological or otherwise – are haunting or preying upon human beings that would explain the dark, gothic affect that is the other aspect of the eerie?

16

In 1977 and 1978 there are many fictions of radical or "alternative" social groups under pressure – undergoing war, deportation, enforced exile. These fictions are not generally very successful (largely because the counter-culture that began in the 60s does not have what it takes to be the basis, or "hero," for a fiction about a group-escape from ordinary reality). Even though it is a part of her *Patternmaster* series, Octavia Butler decides to never bring out a reprint of the novel she writes in 1978 – *Survivor* (she refers to it as her "Star Trek" novel). Ursula Le Guin writes an awkward novel about a group of deported counter-culture protesters living in exile on another planet, *The Eye of the Heron* (the book has many extraordinary moments, but it constitutes a decline from the visionary intensity of books such as *The Left Hand of Darkness*, *The Lathe of Heaven* and *The Word for World is Forest*). *Blake's Seven* will only really save itself as a series by ditching the initial centrality of counter-culture characters (including Blake) and foregrounding a curiously sympathetic Shakespearian machiavel called Avon. It is only really in the extraordinary strange tale of 1977, *The Illearth War*, that there is a degree of success with this focus on an embattled counter-culture.

The question of the strange tale points in a specific direction – toward Oxford and the new breakthrough that occurred 250 years after Shakespeare.

First there is Alice. Then there is Lucy – another girl dreamed up by an Oxford writer who goes through a doorway where there should have been a concrete surface. From the logico-surrealism of Alice to the surreal lucidity of Lucy in the Sky with Diamonds. And from Alice serenely in the strangeness on the other side of the mirror to Lucy in the distorted high-realist world of Narnia (where babies do not oneirically become pigs, but where humans can be turned into stone).

But the story has barely started (and is about to leave behind Oxford completely). In France in 1975 Louis Malle becomes fascinated by the Alice books, and with Joyce Bunuel and Ghislain Uhry creates the eerie futural film *Black Moon*, set in a world where a brutal war is taking place between men and women. In this film a young woman – played by the 16 year-old English actress Cathryn Harrison – escapes from a terrain where military combat is taking place by driving her car into a remote area of French countryside: eventually she continues on foot, and somehow she slips sideways into a world where the conditions of ordinary reality do not apply (Louis Malle says that the Alice books that were a primary inspiration for the film). The film is a striking counterpart to the film of *Picnic at Hanging Rock*, made in the same year (another film which is about a flight across a dimensional boundary from the horror of ordinary reality: the girl in Black Moon is the equivalent of Miranda).

* * *

My own experiences in 1978 were about falling in love with an island-terrain called "Britain", and with a Place in the vicinity of its east coast (terrains and Places are entirely distinct from territories, or human social domains), and simultaneously about starting to fall in love, without any chance of getting anywhere, with a series of girls encountered at the hotels (the girl Colleen, at the Talbot; the girl at the Black Swan).

Looking back on it, it is as if myself and my mother conspired in a long process of foregrounding connections to the *world*, as opposed to human kudos-systems, a process which - after having not been at school in New Zealand – was one of ensuring that I would reach "adulthood" without having fully received any of the markings of my tribe. I was, of course, marked, as normal, with a whole set of initial "anglo-western-world" evaluations, and inculcated directions and biases, but these other markings tended to be slightly displaced, perhaps sometimes a little internationalised, and perhaps sometimes a little too "dreamy" and earnest.

This process would lead to me arriving at things from oblique angles. When I started trying to have relationships with girls I had very few experiences in common with them (with the girl in Helmsley we had modernist pop-rock in common, but I knew nothing at all about punk). I began to dream my way toward the girls I met – toward them and toward their lives, which seemed to have been so different from my own.

The dream of going to university and studying arrived for the first time, so far as I remember, one day when I was on a country road in Northumberland, probably around 1980 (the memory is of suddenly feeling – in advance – the joy of having a room in a hall of residence with a desk at which to study): but a little later than this, when I was living near Malton, I remember noticing girls who were leaving for the university term, or coming back from it, and recurrently finding them very attractive. And at the same time I found their *lives* very attractive: the whole doubleness of a fascinating academic and social life at university, and then of coming home to a beautiful area, and of having the affection there of family and friends.

The becoming-woman involved in this double attraction was in every sense a vital aspect of me, but the two-sided dreamy desire to be at university and to be "rooted" in the English counytryside feels disturbingly more conservative than anything that was overtly in effect within me in 1978. By this time – probably around 1983 – everything had changed. The oneiric-abstract counter-culture – with an internationalism powerfully disseminated, for instance, by Yoko Ono and John Lennon – had been pushed back. The Falklands War had brought patriotism back into the foreground. New, traditionalist fictions had started to appear, fictions set in Oxford and Cambridge: the TV version of *Brideshead Revisited,* and *Chariots of Fire. Tinker, Tailor's* line of light toward an eerie, libidinalised perception of England did not stop it from at the same time being a profound vector of traditionalism, with its end-credits view of Oxford put alongside its newly written "Catholic mass" music, sung by a choir boy, and with its culmination in the shooting of the dark deterritorialised individual – the entirely unsympathetic spy-villain, Bill Haydon (instead of internationalism the vilification of the idea of those who are deterritorialised). This death prefigures that of John Lennon, a few months later.

But if ever I had any kind of positive encounter with a bright, attractive girl I was always instantly on the edge of being in love with her. My yearning in this way to be in a love relationship was the fundamental, central aspect of me – it was then, when this happened, that I felt everything would begin.

But what *is* this yearning? At the deepest and widest level (the level of Love-and-Freedom – of the adventure of existence) in desperately longing to be in love with a girl *who exactly* was I yearning for?

(and an adequate horizon for answering this question can only be provided by reaching an understanding of the strange tale).

* * *

At its most striking (and insofar as it has a fully developed first and second world) the strange tale has a second world which is unlocalisable in relation to the first world, and which could in fact even be taking up the same space. It also has – or at the very least emphatically suggests – a relationship of ongoing inter-action taking place between the two worlds.

What is fundamental about the strange tale is that it figures or delineates an aspect of the world. This aspect is what can be called "the second sphere of action" (where this second sphere is in some sense "superimposed" across the first one).

A description can be given – a kind of phenomenological description – of the way in which the second sphere of action is likely to be seen. Taking this entire account as tentative, and exploratory in its details, the following appear to be the main features of this second sphere:

There is a tendency to see everything in terms of intent (where intent relates to degrees and modalities of freedom, energy, lucidity, love, awareness, feeling, dreaming, abstract-perception, control-fixation, etc), and to act effectively, to some extent at least, on the basis of this perception of the world.

There is a much smaller presence of human beings, and there is a larger presence of animals.

There is a greater awareness of the planet.

There is a recurrent feature that could either be to one side, or in front: it can be seen as either a wall of white light, or a wall of yellow fog. This cloudy light-wall has an eerie, calmly teeming aliveness: it is the wall of the unknown but knowable, but in particular the unknown-but-knowable that is close to you.

There is a centrality – in an active, functional way – of everything that pertains to women, the female, the feminine.

Perception is heightened, and so is abstract perception, and this in part expresses itself as flashes of "seeing": sudden, often very visual graspings of the nature of a situation, or aspect of the world.

There is an ongoing/recurrent process of acquiescing to the *felt*, dream-like promptings of what can be called "Love-and-Freedom," promptings that recurrently have the form of an intense longing which at the same time is an opening up of a direction for bringing about what is longed-for.

There is a sensation of "speeding"– a kind of calm but very

charged sensation of speed, a feeling, most specifically, of a lot being grasped, and being in effect, all at once.

The basis for this tentative account is my own experiences. However most of these features are given a direct description in *The Eagle's Gift*, by Castaneda (1981), and in Florinda Donner's *Being in Dreaming*.

It is also all deeply consonant with *A Thousand Plateaus* (which seems to have been written alongside, or within, the second sphere of action), where for instance there is the description of the transcendental "white wall" which turns out to not be a wall, but an inorganic space of intensities screened with an illusion of absence, so that this screen must be pierced – the wall must be "traversed":

> Go through the wall [...] and at what cost? At the cost – or by the means – of a *becoming-animal, a becoming-flower or rock, and most of all by means of a becoming-imperceptible, a becoming-hard which in fact all along is a becoming with love*. It's a question of speed, even when the speed is that of a "stationery voyage." [26] (my translation).

In *The Eagle's Gift* – published a year after *A Thousand Plateaus* – Castaneda delineates a state of awareness that is called "the second attention", a state whose events are initially very hard to remember (one of the early chapters of the book is called "Quasi Memories of the Other Self"), and the following passage describes a feature of the world that is encountered in the second attention:

> I remembered that once I was with Don Juan and another man whose face I could not remember. The three of us were talking about something I was perceiving as a feature of the world. It was [...] an inconceivable bank of yellowish fog that, as far as

I could tell, divided the world in two. It went from the ground up to the sky, to infinity. While I talked to the two men, the half of the world to my left was intact and the half to my right was veiled in fog. [...] Don Juan made me turn a few degrees to my right, and I saw that the wall of fog moved as I turned my head. The world was divided in two at a level my intellect could not comprehend. [...].

The other man said that it was a great accomplishment to divide the world in two, but it was an even greater accomplishment when a warrior had the serenity and control to stop the rotation of that wall. He said that the wall was not inside us; it was certainly out in the world, dividing it in two... [...]. The great accomplishment of keeping the wall from turning enabled the warrior to face the wall and gave him the power to go through it any time he so desired. [27]

The point of greatest intensity and lucidity in the strange tale during this time is *The Illearth War*. The story *The Quiet Man*, by John Foxx (1980) delineates many of the aspects of the second sphere of action, but it is the eerie journey into the mountains in the centre of Donaldson's trilogy that goes furthest in this direction.

The terrain – a very large area of mountains – is devoid of people, apart from the five who set out into it. For many chapters the group meets no-one. And when at the end of the events they do meet someone, in a cavern deep beneath a mountain where "the blood of the earth" flows from a crack, it is a spectral entity, seen initially "through the stone, rather than within the cave." It is rare in a book that an absence of people is foregrounded so effectively, and unobtrusively. As in real experiences in a wilderness, after a while the silence becomes insistent, a visceral presence.

Animals are foregrounded because the group really consists of four humans (Elena, Covenant, Bannor, Morin) an anomalous being called Amok, one ordinary horse, and three "Ranhyn" horses. "Ranhyn" belong to a population of horses that are at a higher level of development than other horses. They cannot be tamed, and are allies of humans rather than servants: on rare occasions they choose a human to be their rider. Toward the end of the journey Elena's female Ranhyn dies in a rockfall saving the ordinary horse. And the centrality of the Ranhyn is not removed when the horses are left behind to travel down into the mountain. To reach Earthroot (where water flows which gives 'the Power of Command') the five people have to cross a wide subterranean lake in a boat that comes toward them across the lake – the boat is an expression of what is called "Earthpower" – and which will then only move across the lake if its occupants speak. Elena chooses to propel the boat by telling the story of what happened when as a child her Ranhyn took her to a meeting of all the Ranhyn horses in a distant valley far to the south of the place where she lived.

The presence of the planet is at a higher intensity for several reasons. There is no human social world around the group: there is the insistent presence of the mountains, and the mountains are features of the planet. And it is not just the rock of the planet that is emphasised. There is also a subtle, and powerful emphasis on the sky: the place toward which the group travels is a high mountain with twin peaks – and with a plateau around it on the east– called Melenkurion *Skyweir* [my italics]. The group is travelling from the northeast, on the outer edge of the border of the lands in which the events all take place, and when they arrive at the centre of the plateau, and are looking west to the mountain and the sky between the peaks, they are looking toward the *outside* – they are looking toward the uncharted "beyond". From the direction of the outside the sky – the wind – can flow between the peaks, which are the "skyweir" for the river of the unknown.

But the planet is most intensely foregrounded by the fact that the journey is toward a place where "Earthpower' is concentrated, and Earthpower here is very definitely something that pertains to the "body without organs" of the planet – it belongs to the world of intent, lucidity, creativity. The boat on the subterranean lake is an expression of Earthpower.

Women, the female and the feminine are involved, in an intensely active, dynamic way, on more than one level. Elena is by far the most powerful of the members of the group, because she is the pre-eminent master in "the Land" of a pragmatic, anomalous knowledge called "lore" that is used for the purposes of creation, nurture and combat. She is the "high lord" of the small group of lore-masters whose role it is to defend the Land. She is also attractive, and in love with Covenant, this highlighting her as feminine, to a greater extent than if she was solely a warrior lore-master defending her society.

But there is no doubt left by the book that Earthpower is female – that the planet itself is female. On the far side of the lake there is a narrow tunnel, with a tiny stream of red fluid flowing down the centre. They walk along this tunnel and arrive after a short time in a small cave (Covenant is in anguished state because he is afraid of what will happen to Elena):

He squeezed the water out of his eyes, gained a moment in which to make out his surroundings. He stood behind Elena in a wider cave at the tunnel's end. Before him, set into the black stone end-wall like an exposed lode-facet, was a rough, sloping plane of wet rock. […] It confronted him like a porous membrane in the foundation of time and space. From top to bottom, it bled moisture which dripped down the slope, collected in a rude trough, and flowed away along the centre of the tunnel.

"Behold," Amok said quietly. "Behold the Blood of the Earth."[28]

The place at the centre of this "zone" – using the term in the sense derived from the film Stalker – is evidently a kind of planetary vagina, a "cosmic vagina." The female could barely be more foregrounded in this world – it is the ground itself, and the sky. And this would be true even without the connection to "the lady of the lake" brought about by the similarity of circumstances (the need for assistance in a war) and the way in which the boat being mysteriously propelled is the equivalent of the appearance of the sword, in the Arthurian mythos.

This in turn leads to the way in which the whole of the mountain becomes a "figuring" of the strangest feature of the second sphere of action: the transcendental "cloud of unknowing" that is the wall of fog, or the wall of light.

When the group arrives at Melenkurion Skyweir they are travelling south, and the mountain, as they go to the centre of the plateau, is on their right. To their right is where the river of the sky is flowing toward them, from the unknown lands to the west. And when they do succeed, after a struggle lasting days, in getting into the mountain (turning to the right) they are rapidly confronted by an anomalous "doorway," which is a space between a rock wall and a stalactite in which, at a touch from Amok (who is an intensely unknown or enigmatic being, equivalent to Ariel in *The Tempest*, as well as Puck) a space of coloured light appears:

A fine yellow filigree network began to grow in the air. Starting from Amok's fingertip, the delicate web of light spread outward in the plane of the gap. Like a skein slowly crystallising into visibility, it expanded until it filled the whole Door. [… He] stepped briskly through the web.

He did not break the delicate strands of light. Rather, he disappeared as he touched them. Covenant could see no trace of him on the ledge beyond the Door. [...] Morin followed Amok. He, too, vanished as he came in contact with the yellow web.[29]

The "wall" or "cloud" is also being evinced or figured at the point where the group reaches the cave beyond the lake and stare toward the plane of rock with the fluid streaming down it:

> This whole plane shimmered; its emanations distorted his ineffectual vision, gave him the impression that he was staring at a mirage, a wavering in the solid stuff of existence.[30]

* * *

It is vital to say at this point that to turn to face the wall of light – the wall of fog – is to stop seeing the world of existence at higher and higher levels of intensity as being some other direction in relation to that of the Future. In fact the future as ordinarily conceived is the chronic future of deadened, trapped existence with all its pathological fixations on "semi-frozen", denuded, predictable processes. It is necessary to see that the wall of light *is* fundamentally the future - so that it has been brought round to the south, where the ordinary-world, "deadened-anticipation" future had been, giving the view in the direction of the futural valleys of time, the valleys of the Future - (the second sphere of action is in fact the first of these valleys).

It was where you were looking before – the "chronic" future – that was the place to the side, the "sideshow". A deadly sideshow that distracts you toward your death. In contrast, in the direction of the Future is the planet, women, dreams, animals, birds, the sky – all of the brightness and creativity of the cosmos, all of the intent-currents. This is *South*, the Future.

* * *

It feels as if Virginia Woolf wrote *The Waves* as a result of sustained experiences of seeing the second sphere of action (the strange tale has liminal forms as well as explicit ones, and some of these border-line instances are among the most powerful, as with both *The Waves*, and *Picnic at Hanging Rock*). The passages that begin each section are each a description of a depopulated world, with birds and trees and plants, and a house by the sea with almost no-one around. The wall of fog is the sky and the sea, and the mirror in the house is like a detached fragment of this wall:

The sun rose. Bars of yellow and green fell on the shore, gilding the ribs of the eaten-out boat and making the sea-holly and its mailed leaves gleam blue as steel. Light almost pierced the thin swift waves as they raced fan-shaped over the beach. The girl who had shaken her head and made all the jewels, the topaz, the aquamarine, the water-coloured jewels, dance, now bared her brows and with wide-opened eyes drove a straight pathway over the waves. [...]

In the garden the birds that had sung erratically and spasmodically in the dawn on that tree, on that bush, now sang together in chorus, shrill and sharp; now together, as if conscious of companionship, now alone as if to the pale blue sky. [...]

Now, too, the rising sun came in at the window, touching the red-edged curtain, and began to bring out circles and lines. Now in the growing light its whiteness settled in the plate; the blade condensed its gleam. Chairs and tables loomed behind so that though each was separate they seemed inextricably involved. The looking glass whitened its pool upon the wall.[31]

* * *

In the context of my own experiences in 1978, this account of the second sphere of action has in part been aimed at providing a way of thinking about what is really happening when a young man is yearning to be *in love* with a girl. Everyone thinks they know all about this, and yet perhaps nothing is more recondite.

Who was I looking for?

It is obvious I was looking for Elena. It is obvious I was searching for Miranda from *Picnic at Hanging Rock* (who leads her group of women up the Rock on a journey of escape), and that I was also searching for the girl from Black Moon. I was looking for the shared, interfused bliss of a dance of becomings. And inseparably I was looking for a woman who would be a lucid, courageous explorer of the unknown – a woman with whom I could depart toward the second sphere of action.

But of course, to ask a truly gothic question, *who else would I have been looking for*? Who else would I have been looking for, assuming you put to one side the domain – visible over your shoulder in the wall of fog – of imposed, extrinsic desires?

17

There was *another* area in Yorkshire on which our journeys centred in that first year of hotel-nomadism, from October 1977 to November 1978. This was also the area where we settled in a rented house for four months at the end of the year, for the winter which turned out to be the coldest for 27 years, and which would also turn out to be the strike-riddled end of the Labour administration, "the winter of discontent". This, broadly speaking, was the area around Otley, Ilkley and Bradford to the south, stretching up along the valleys of the Wharfe and Aire rivers past (and including) Grassington and Skipton to relatively remote areas in the "Dales" country of Upper Wharfedale.

When I returned from New Zealand I was met at Heathrow by my mother (myself and my 17 year-old sister had just spent a year living entirely "unsupervised," during which we had both got full-time jobs).) After a night at a hotel by the airport the first place we stayed in Yorkshire was a modern hotel about five miles south of Otley, in a village called Bramhope. This village was at the northern tip of a conurbation's ribbon-development that reached like a finger from the centre of Leeds. The tip of the "finger" – consisting of upper middle-class, leafy-lanes houses – looked out over the green expanses of the middle part of Wharfedale. Perhaps the first trip we made, maybe the day after our arrival, was to some friends of my mother's who lived on a farm sixty miles away in a village called Fadmoor, over in the North York Moors, maybe 10 miles from Helmsley. However, even though we never once stayed in the centre of Leeds, we perhaps stayed 5 times at that hotel in the course of that year (and maybe 10 times in the entire two and a half years of living in hotels).

(A year later we would settle in a rented holiday cottage – a "winter let" it was called – in a small village near Skipton. There had in fact been an earlier attempt to rent a house – for the winter – that was on a hill a few miles west of Malton).

This other area extended north from my mother's place of origin, Bradford. It almost entirely consisted of countryside, though with largish towns such as Ilkley and Skipton, and had its own limestone beauty and grandeur in and around the last twenty miles of Wharfedale. However, although I really liked this terrain, and found it enjoyably atmospheric in all its different regions, there was *something* that was very much not the same about this entire area, in comparison with the North York Moors and the places around them. A bleakness, a faint *greyness*, in comparison, something so intangible that – although I was aware of it – I would have had difficulty giving any sort of adequate explanation.

The difference in intensity perhaps only really began to make itself felt around the "turn" of the summer, as the year climbed up into August. There was a difference in intensity in myself – in the "background" I was now slightly perturbed, deintensified, and the energy of summer was beginning to recede. I was very much looking forward to winter, and yet nonetheless a melancholy "edge" began to appear in my experiences. And this new bleak, recurring tone was very much associated with the area to the west.

It was not at all as simple as there being no equivalent of the double secludedness of the wide, hill-shielded "vale" with the hidden valleys beyond it (there were even features that in some ways were similar). The vital fact was that – to a far greater extent than was the case with the valleys and hills around the Rye river – the area was a zone of devastation created by the linked industries of factory textile production and sheep farming. What this means is that the upper valleys of the Wharfe and Aire rivers were almost entirely without trees – they were bleak, denuded landscapes. The terrain was a remorselessly "industrial" sheep-farming zone that had for centuries been plugged directly into the areas to the south where factories had produced textiles from the wool. The tops of the hills in the North York Moors have in fact also been entirely stripped of their trees, but, as has already been pointed out, the valleys, lower slopes and other adjoining areas to the south and southwest have a large amount of woodland.

The difference concerned is not simply a question of a comparison between two areas. I have a very clear, intense memory of setting out early on a hot summer morning on my bicycle from Northallerton (a town in between the two areas) and of being astonished by the beauty of the places through which I was cycling, all of which were areas where woodland formed the majority of the horizon. That day I cycled around seventy miles to Hexham in Northumberland – and it was on one occasion when my mother and I travelled into the hills southwest of Hexham (which was one of the places in the third area in northern England which we visited a lot in that year) that I saw perhaps the most attractive hidden valley I have ever seen in Britain, and that valley, though surrounded by bare moorland, had a large number of trees.

It was not that I was unhappy in the western "haunt" of Yorkshire. I was recurrently neurotic wherever I was, but neurosis is bound up with happiness (joy is on a level beyond happiness, and in fact I experienced a lot of joy in all the phases and terrains of that year). It was more that a new tone was beginning to appear on the edge of things, or to flicker into existence for a moment.

The Anchor Hotel was by the side of the Leeds/Liverpool canal in a village called Gargrave, which is five miles from Skipton (it was also two miles away from the village where later we would live for four months). The valley of the Aire is very wide in the area of Skipton and Gargrave – maybe three miles across, and remaining quite wide for many miles to the north (it is never anything like as broad for the whole of the river's onward course through the urbanised and industrialised Pennine valleys to the south). But this terrain, despite it being an attractive "vale", is largely devoid of trees, as are the relatively high hills that rise up from it to the northeast and southwest (it is the centre of a region which is called "Craven" – the local paper is the "Craven Herald").

And the Anchor hotel – an unprepossessing roadside place in the middle of this somewhat denuded landscape – had a feature that for me had an enigmatically powerful, melancholy effect. This feature was a series of four or five paintings in the upstairs corridors.

They were clichéd, washily stylised pictures of pre-dusk or twilight beaches with two or three minimally rendered outline-figures in the near to middle distance (perhaps the figures were made from only two or three brush-strokes) and with a few sailboats and an unusually coloured sky, perhaps an amber-orange colour in one case. The figures were spaced out from each other, and because the sky was an indeterminate area of colour it was not necessarily clear whether cloud or clear sky was being shown (although they did not show the sun – if the sky was cloud it was being lit from behind by the sun).

Looking at these paintings filled me with a sharply poignant, dream-like state of melancholy, a state that was surprisingly sustained (I could get the experience again and again), and which although achingly sad was also inseparably a feeling of joy – or joy in the form of longing. I became one of the figures – or all of them – and I became a feeling, a time, a dreamed haunting event. I knew there was a connection for me with my sister, and to a superficial extent with a memory of a 90 mile (round trip) cycle-ride the two of us had done to a beautiful bay called Akaroa – one day during a weekend when we were living in New Zealand on our own. However, the places and the feelings were not at all suggestive of Akaroa, and in any case, everything was *futural*: the dream to which I was taken was in the future. It was like a short story, a tale, but where I was deeply identified with it: the feeling or idea was something like "at last we are together, but it's too late..." or "we can't pretend we can come closer again, the way we were years ago, but for this moment, while it lasts, we're together...". Another aspect that separated it from the past, and from any obvious familial reference, was that the figures in the "dream" were of roughly the same age, and even though I was reminded of my sister the relationships had a quality primarily of friendship, but in some way belonging to an *epic*, anguish-strewn domain of friendship.

I had had some experience of abstract and surrealist paintings: in Christchurch I used to stand and look at the window display of an art-shop that specialised in popular, immediately striking areas of modern art, and there were certain surrealist abstract landscapes – with isolated, monolithic forms in a vast expanse - that had moved me in a similar way. So the Anchor Hotel pictures moving me to this degree was not a result of me never having looked closely at "stylised" paintings before. But a curious fact is that I felt at the time not only that it was possible to re-see the paintings in the hotel as somewhat tawdry and formula-based (this was how my mother saw them), but that in assessing them non-holistically I could only agree with this view. Not only that – I am sure I *felt* at the time both that there might be something indulgent, or deleteriously "melancholic"about their effect, and that this effect might even be idiosyncratic in some sense.

I was cut off from my sister, primarily by distance (she had stayed behind in New Zealand, and would not return for another three years) but also by my neurotic tendency to attempt to express as much as possible of my experiences and ideas in writing letters to her, which in practice meant that—I even though I sometimes wrote long letters, I almost never wrote to her. And my sister had been one third of the only group of which I had been a part since I was eight, and was the only person of my own generation with whom I had ever had a sustained relationship.

There is a fundamental difference between melancholy and moments of feeling the background sadness that emanates from the world. Melancholy always has a quality of languor and self-indulgence (and indeterminate, unrecognised self-pity). The background sadness is sharp in its intensity, and comes without indulgence as a wave that hits you, and then leaves you experiencing this aspect of the world as one more stimulus to break free (all those who have gone down in the fight would want you to break free).

* * *

I also remember a time when I was walking in the market square of Skipton, around March of 1979, and I suddenly had this phrase in my head - "it's all been a bit of a waste of time for me, hasn't it?" The phrase came with a "scene" where I was a man who, after a long series of dramatic events, had failed to form a relationship with a woman who had been involved in these events, a woman who instead had come together with another man. It was the end of a story, the end of a fiction – one of the last phrases. It was strikingly melancholy, and it also gave me the feeling that I was remembering a scene in an actual drama I had heard or seen.

The key to understanding the affect involved is of course that it is deep resentment and self-pity disguised as "grand resig-nation", or "heroic equanimity". I think one is always aware of the true nature of these affective (or passive/passional) modes, but nonetheless I found the scene moving. It seemed to be the end of a powerful romantic drama, and it was after all breaking the rules, because it was a romantic drama where the hero does not get the girl (and this form of resentful response is evidently a better response than jealous rage – though of course in reality it might well be the precursor of rage). What is deeply twisted about the phrase is of course that from the point of view of love no time "spent" with the loved individual could ever have been wasted (this idea of waste, and of investment of time is here entirely a construct of the control mind).

The other thing that was enigmatic was that it obliquely reminded me of something from *The Hitchhikers Guide to the Galaxy* (I had heard this programme for the first time on the first day I stayed at The Anchor Hotel): I felt I was remembering something else, and yet the end of the *Hitchhikers Guide to the Galaxy* came to my mind.

In Douglas Adam's story the melancholy subject of the phrase – as it turned out when I checked a few years later – is a caveman, who is not in fact losing a hoped-for girlfriend, but is losing the whole of planet Earth to an invading group of marketing consultants (etc.) who have been ejected from a planet elsewhere in the galaxy. A few lines from the end of the initial series Arthur Dent says to the caveman – "it's all been a bit of a waste of time for you, hasn't it?"

* * *

A primary form in which I experienced joy during that year was in listening to songs on the radio that I had bought (with some of the last of my savings from working in the shop in New Zealand). I remember a road with a view of the summer countryside to the west in a town called Ponteland in Northumberland (my mother's best friend lived in this town), and being blown away by hearing Annie Haslam singing Northern Lights. I remember being similarly blown away by Kate Bush singing Wuthering Heights, just after I bought the radio, in March.

But I have no memories at all of enjoying listening to songs in the "other" area on the west of Yorkshire. Even if I include the four months living in the house near Skipton, I have no recollections of enjoying hearing songs on the radio, let alone recollections of experiencing joy in this way.

In contrast, I have very evocative, *sunlit* memories of being swept away by songs while I was staying at the Talbot Hotel in April.

These memories are centred on listening to songs in my room at the hotel, a room with a view to the southeast across the train station to hills in the distance (all of the other events I remember at the hotel took place when I was staying in other rooms), and walking outside with my radio in the street.

All of the memories share the same quality of listening to *the party*. Being tuned to the perpetual party of pop-rock's lightness, joy, and freedom from sententious and religious gravity. The Future – life at a higher degree of intensity – was evidently there all along. To know this, you just had to turn on the radio (or look at the sunlit hills in the distance).

The song that blew me away in Malton, in the spring of 1978 was Automatic Lover, by Dee. D. Jackson, with her dispassionately and yearningly keening refrain "See me, hear me, feel me /Love me, touch me..."

To a certain extent this song needs to be seen as an after-shock following Donna Summer's I Feel Love, the year before, but its relatively limited success in the UK was probably partly the result of poor presentation on Top of the Tops. The song reached number four in the UK, but it was number 1 in Italy, France, Spain, Argentina, Turkey and Japan. I didn't know anything about this at the time (I probably heard the song only three or four times) – I just knew there was love and a kind of eerie and blissful sensuality in Dee. D. Jackson's voice.

As far as I am aware I had never heard "I Feel Love". It was probably a little too viscerally extreme to be a huge hit in a New Zealand that was in love with ABBA, and the first time I remember being transfixed by it was at some point in the early 2000s, when I believed I was hearing a recent remix of a song from the sixties (I did not in the least associate the song with "disco"), only to discover shortly afterwards that I had been hearing the original, and that the song was understood to be the beginning of disco (rather than disco being understood as a pale, miserably flamboyant "tracing" of its intensity).

This whole experience with the delayed impact of "I Feel Love" is striking, given that the song was the "future" track from a concept album whose tracks represented past present and future. However, for now, while pointing out its sheer untimely beauty, it is important also to say that it does in fact – unavoidably – contain an element that will be nothing but helpful for the stratificatory processes that will reconfigure this mode of being into something bleakly erotic. It is as dangerous to connect love with *feeling* as to connect it with self-sacrifice: love is a flight or blissful becoming consisting of creativity, inter-awareness, dance and metamorphosis (and feeling for the control mind has been connected up with hedonism and eroticism as opposed to the non-selfish and blissful escape of being in love).

Automatic Lover inhabits the same space as Donna Summer's song, and with the same hostage to fortune, only – rather than it representing the future in a concept album – it is a "sci-fi" song. In what feels like an affectionate critique of something geekishly and deceptively low-intensity lurking within Kraftwerk (Jackson had been working as a producer in Munich), there is a computer-voice intoning "I am your automatic lover" and then there is the "coldly" or dispassionately ecstatic woman who is dreaming of an entirely different lover. The melody is hauntingly beautiful and there is a quality of a woman waking from a reason-entrapment in the direction of love, and of a wider reality grasped by lucidity. At the time I heard the song as a sci-fi tale about a female, sentient robot-being that was waking up as an entity, and discovering love and sensuality, like Rachel in Bladerunner, a film that was still four years in the future.

What happened when Dee D. Jackson was swept up into "space disco" is not really relevant here (this is not a criticism – I have not heard any other songs by her). I certainly made no connection at the time between the dull, exuberant funkishness of "Saturday Night Fever" and the delicately ecstatic sci-fi pop-rock of "Automatic Lover'. Listening to the song now, the song's rhythm feels as if it has far more in common with a song like Radioactivity (1975) than with the Bee Gees.

Pop-rock was attempting to escape into conventionally "futural" and ecstatic visions. It was not in any way set up now to go in the direction of the planet, following Joan Lindsay, and the Patti Smith of *Horses*. In March (though I was not aware of her at all at the time) Patti Smith's *Easter* had signalled the beginning of her collapse. Neither sci-fi visions nor disco ecstasy were going to prevent an overall decline in the degree of dreaming of the outside of ordinary, constricted reality.

I was discovering that there were strange and wonderful women singing at the pop-rock party (Annie Haslam, Dee.D Jackson, Kate Bush). And without me being aware of it I was discovering that in the vicinity of the North York Moors (as opposed to the area around Skipton and Ilkley) it was easier for me to approach the abstract-oneiric threshold of being consciously and pragmatically in love with the planet.

* * *

What is it to be in the "wrong" place? At the very least it is for there to be somewhere that could be easily reached that would in some sense be substantially better.

However, it is vital to avoid having an "epic" or a "romantic" way of understanding the times when the Future is predominantly nearer to zones of the human social world. What is over the boundary is not less dangerous than ordinary reality – the second sphere of action might even be *more* dangerous. Also, these times of greater proximity are to be understood as something like traps for those who are drawn forward, and who then crash and burn, in one way or another. It is not for instance that the heroic human "zeitgeist" keeps getting closer to crossing a threshold. On the contrary there is a kind of chronic-time disaster taking place (chronic-time is the direction of overall human progression and is an utterly different direction from that of the Future) – a disaster or fixation-entrapment in which human beings are being pushed further and further away from lucidity, and therefore from a focused state of love and exploration.

18

When I arrived in Malton in late July of 2013 it was thirty five years later. And – as I worked out on the coach on the way up – it was twenty years since the last time I had been there. It was around four-thirty in the afternoon, and I went to a small Asda that had appeared alongside the train station to get some supplies for four days of walking. After a delay in a Malton side-street caused by the need to fit the shopping into my backpack – alongside a small supermarket that had once been called Jackson Grandways, but was now called Sainsbury's – I set off along the road that leads to Hovingham, and then to Helmsley.

I was not prepared for how moved I was going to be. The process of writing this book (I had started it three months before) had made my return a very charged and "focused" event, and maybe I should have known. But there were no pre-tremors – it was only as I was walking along the road, in late afternoon sunlight.

During that walk I kept getting the amorphous idea (with the following specific words) that my mother and myself had contrived to "hide away inside a year", and that for this anomalous escape we had made Helmsley and Malton our "headquarters". I have not been satisfied at any point by the rather grandiose, romanticising tone of this phrase (and it will be necessary to give an account of what was behind the events to remove its bad effect). But the main idea is really that a primary motivation for what happened was the desire to stay away from ordinary reality, with its systems of conventional "judgements" (impositions of deadened existence emergent from fear, resentment and deference to power).

This is all therefore a question of freedom: what took place was the creation of a kind of shelter, or zone of freedom. From my own point of view, within the zone of freedom (and within the limits of what it afforded) there were vast expanses of time during which I was free to do and think whatever I wanted, without human contact that would afflict me with constrictive views. Also, because I dreamed of being a writer the idea – which would have arrived just by thinking and reading – that I was failing to make possible my entry into university had absolutely no effect on me. It was an instinct that going to university had nothing to do with becoming a writer.

However this was a zone of freedom at degree zero. It was constructed from strength of will – primarily on the part of my mother – and out of money created by the previous generation. But it was not a space in which intensificatory, upward-spiralling processes occurred – I was always dreaming up stories, songs, and ideas, and doing drawings, but nothing "took flight" and started to build upon itself. And nor was there anything approaching the strength that would have created new financial resources without a collapse into wage slavery. In the spring of 1979 my mother's money temporarily ran out, and I got a job to support us at a shop in a village that was four miles along the road to Hovingham (I worked there for a year, travelling by bus to and from a rented house in a windswept area five miles in the opposite direction from Malton, to the east). As I walked out of Malton, I was walking initially toward a place where I had worked during a recurrently bleak, difficult year.

* * *

In one sense my mother's life in 1978 had become one of being "over-faced" by her circumstances: the result of a combination of distress about a difficult family situation, and the loneliness that caused her to travel across England and Wales to visit her friends. She had a solicitor in Newcastle who was working on contesting the legality of the will that had been accepted as her father's on his death (he had died in 1976), and this was behind some of her trips to Northumberland. Her week-by-week aims and preoccupations fell into this overall field of contesting the will, visiting friends, and phases when her intentions (which evidently to a great extent were rationalisations) were about recuperation, completing small practical tasks, and looking for a house.

But at another level what took place during all of that time was to do with the fact that my mother had discovered the pleasure of hotel nomadism. She had done it for a year on her own, already, and now had my company. I recurrently felt acutely frustrated by being trapped on this bizarre parental bus, but I also enjoyed the travelling and the countryside and the hotels.

My mother was a very intelligent and courageous woman – a lucid, thoughtful feminist, and generally a non-conformist, with a strong interest in science and sociology – but her life had become fundamentally *blocked*. A kind of quiet, fiercely debilitating depression had taken her over in New Zealand, as a result of a failed marriage, bringing up two children on her own, and the shutting down of her career. She had a qualification from an agricultural college, as well as a sociology degree, and had emigrated to New Zealand only to be told, emphatically, that the jobs for which she was qualified in the agricultural world were never given to women.

When I returned from New Zealand myself and my sister had packed up most of the furniture and belongings in the house and sent it back to Britain, and I arrived back with a power-of-attorney form for my mother to sign – I hoped – in order for my sister to sell the house. My mother refused to sign the form because she did not want to give this power to the solicitor.

* * *

I had a realisation a few years ago – in an hour-long process that came from nowhere, and that involved a lot of near-hypnotic recall – about what had happened in New Zealand, one that was similar to the experience this summer (although it came with images rather than words, and left me with no feeling of a "tinge" of something sentimental). I saw that during 6 years in New Zealand my mother my sister and myself had "made a stand" against conventional existence. An easily explicable initiator of this event (although very much only one aspect) was that my mother wanted to return to Britain, but did not want my sister and myself to have any contact with our father, who – probably for good reasons – she intensely disliked and distrusted (she had divorced him, emigrated to New Zealand, and officially changed all of our names, in order to prevent any contact). It can also be said that my mother at the beginning of this time registered my sister and myself onto a "correspondence course" for our school education, which then as it turned out we never took, so that what really happened was that we had no further school education.

My mother was the shield that bore the brunt of the effects of being drawn into taking a stand of this kind, and I think her subsequent tendency to be an insomniac who was slowed down in practical matters – though never in thought and conversation – and who was addicted to indulgent nomadic procrastinations, was the result of the misery she went through during the six years in New Zealand where everything for her children "fell apart upwards" into a school-free existence. During this time my sister and myself quietly ran wild (it was necessary to be inconspicuous because of the danger of the "authorities" being called in to shut down our freedom). But for my mother that time became a kind of lonely stasis.

Given that she was in love with the British countryside, travelling around it with me was a much better situation than being stuck in a house in a state of paralysed exile (my sister and myself both fell in love with New Zealand, but the combination of greater sexism in the society and deep unhappiness prevented this from happening with our mother). In 1978 she was experiencing her life in many ways as a series of daunting challenges and distressing events (this is the main thing she would have talked about if asked). And yet nonetheless that year was, I suspect, one of the better years in her life since everything had started to go wrong for her in the 1960s.

* * *

And – again – what about the overall situation in 1978? What *was* this year in which my mother and myself were on the run from conventional existence, profligately burning up a stash of previous-generation wealth?

A vital background fact is that approximately eighty to a hundred years before there had been a change – in the "western" world – in the organisation of the system of reason-revelation. The change was from revelation being pre-eminent in relation to reason to the opposite. In a polarity reversal (which in fact functions to push everyone even further away from lucidity than they were before) the discourses of science and rationality came out on top over the discourses of revelation, in that it became clear that it was no longer legitimate, in any social, political or academic forum, to use beliefs taken from religion to attempt to disprove a scientific position, or to use arguments to attempt to prove a religious view. On the contrary, the new instinctive presupposition was that it would be laughable to attempt such things. Those who had opposed Bishop Wilberforce's mockery in the evolution debate of 1860 had very definitely had the last laugh.

But the new form of reason-revelation is just as much a system as the old one. The point-of-connection between the two sides is thought that functions along the lines of Hegel, where a rational modality is employed to construct – fallaciously interpret –

historical change as having all been a globalised movement of "mind" or "spirit" toward the end-point of love (although love which is not understood as what it is), and where the Bible can be construed allegorically in endless ways to fit in with this picture. And there is now an associated tendency for violence and cruelty in their different forms to be understood through psychology and psychoanalysis, rather than through the discourse of "evil." If it has all been a dialectical movement of progress there is room only for confusion and madness in the story (this change in itself is an improvement, but it is connected to a suppression of lucidity, and a blocked, progress-bedtime-story perspective on what is taking place in the human world).

Probably the vast majority of scientists remain religious at some level or another (to say nothing of the reason-cult's recurrent mystic philosophy of Platonic metaphysics). Scientists and social theorists start out as pre-eminently rationalist radicals and recurrently their religion comes to the foreground as they get older (in general for an individual an emplaced religious dreaming can only finally be replaced by another one, or by a free, non-transcendence dreaming or perspective – a free oneiric-abstract perceiving of the world). In relation to the polarity-reversal, on one level – the level of control-mind dismissive or suppressive metaphysics – all that has happened is a change within the functioning of those who say '"it's all just...". Those who might say "it's all just the physical world, or the laws of nature" are now dominant discursively over those who might say "it's all just the will of God."

Modernism, in its primary current sense – as opposed to the expanded sense that includes the modernist "precursors", such as Shakespeare – is an emergence of oneiric-abstract worlds that functioned as part of what triggered the change in the system of reason-revelation, and at the same time is the work that continued along new lines after this change in circumstances in relation to the control-mind (there is a broader sense of the term that can be used for all of the movements toward wider realities – and toward freedom – from which the artworks emerge).

What really took place was that, under pressure, the system of reason-revelation used some of the force of a push toward freedom to alter its grip to a more oppressive one (more oppressive because it has pushed people even further away from lucidity). It remains the case that immense gains were made in many fundamental respects in relation to freedom (though the pushing of everyone further away from lucidity – and therefore from dreamings and becomings – unfortunately more than counteracts the gains, overall).

The higher-intensity phase that started around 1962 was not the first since the change. But it was the first where dreamings that were an expression of the lightness of the Outside (and that included a challenge to the gravity of religion) went right through the whole social field. Very few people had read *The Waves*, but almost everyone listened to the Beatles.

* * *

What was eerie about 1978 was that it was the calm before the collapse. It was the sunlit, expansive moment of "this far toward the outside, but how to go further, with the tide turning?" Of course, this only relates to the ways in which people had been turned toward the Future, or had set out to go there: in most respects everything in a phase of higher-intensity is very much the same as "normal" (a world of oppressed people fixated on things like football, and who behave as if they will live forever, because everyone behaves like this, and because the ambient background view is that in another sense everyone will – as "immortal souls").

Although I had no ability to bring all this into focus, there was a tone or quality I kept hearing at the time. I remember cycling on a sunny day across some moorland in County Durham and having this song in my head (I only knew the first two lines, and I didn't know the band) –

Davy's on the road again, wearing different clothes again
Davy's turning handouts down to keep his pockets clean
All his goods are sold again, his word's as good as gold again
Sez if you see Jean now tell her to pity me

As I now know the band was Manfred Mann's Earth Band, who musically were a kind of continuation of the 60s (like Fleetwood Mac, but much less talented). I really liked the song, but there was something melancholy about it. Davy was on the road, which felt very good: but there was something wrong, or "doomy" about this journey.

Earlier, in March, there had been the sadness of Baker Street. I liked the song, but I was aware of its gentle, slightly languorous melancholy (I never concentrated on the words at all, but it wasn't necessary):

this city desert makes me feel so cold…
I used to think that it was so easy…
another year and I'll be happy…
but who's crying now?

The song ends with "you're goin' home" (the "lad" who is encountered within the narrative of the song – described as "the rolling stone," and as continually failing to do what he wants to do – is about to be left behind in the sunlight of a "new morning"). And in summer the woman in the song Northern Lights had been off on a journey, but now she is renouncing travelling in favour of "destination homeward bound, take the easy way, take me down".

1978 was a sunlit world of the pop-rock party – the brightening dawn of the future – and yet why was the world of film obsessed with disasters of every kind? Why did I find *The Shining* such a realistic book? Why all the deeply melancholic philosophy in *The Hitch-Hiker's Guide to the Galaxy*? (a philosopher in the series lives on his own in a hut on a desolate planet, and is occasionally visited by people in spaceships; at one point someone begins to tell the entire truth of the world as a result of a court-room truth–drug, and a concrete bunker is built around the court-room).

It was not that the songs I was hearing were poor but were being treated as good. The next year listening to The Police I would feel that way – I would feel that the songs were genuinely innovative but were somehow grey and uninspired. In 1978 it was more that the songs were hauntedly bright. A brightness haunted by sadness.

There was something around at that time that was like a faint dark shadow (it had nothing to do with melancholy). I remember being at a hotel in the centre of Ilkley in September, and there was a gas explosion, during the middle of the night, in a shop on the high street, around 300 yards from the hotel (the shop was destroyed). I slept through the explosion, but I remember getting a strange jolt from the event – a jolt which did not have anything to do with any ordinary state of fear in relation to physical danger. I know that it reminded me of the explosion of the boiler in *The Shining* (the boiler is "the thing that has been forgotten"), and that would have been enough to give me a shiver, given I was living in hotels. But it was more than that. And I don't think it is enough to speculate that it was a reminder of my death. It was a silent explosion (I had not heard it) that jolted me in an eerie way, a bit like the young Louis hearing the chained beast stamping on the beach in *The Waves* (and what would the boiler be if it was within a human being?). I sense that as much as it was a reminder of death, it was a reminder of power.

(power in this context is a neutral term, bringing together the idea of energy with that of will or intention).

Reading *The Shining* through the night in an old hotel had been a very frightening experience, and a noticeable coincidence, even if it was a coincidence that was likely to occur, under the circumstances. Later, during the extreme winter of that year there would be another coincidence of a similar kind. But that was six months away. The time I am thinking about now was September, the month before the broadcast of the TV version of *No-Mans Land* (Oct. 3rd).

It was in September that *Systems of Romance* was released, the inconspicuously haunted album by the Ultravox that had John Foxx as its singer (I did not hear it until many years later).

This album takes place on the edge of an "outside" which is recurrently figured as the world beyond a window. But it is clear the window is really a "gap" in the direction of the unknown – an unknown which is preternaturally calm, high-energy and silent, and which is encountered through perception, through memory-worlds, and through pictures and photographs. This is from the first song, Slow Motion:

"Pictures, I've got pictures, and I run them in my head.
When I can't sleep at night
Looking out at the white world and the moon
I feel a soft exchange taking place
Merging with the people on the frames..." ( )

The liminal place by the window is one where the world is experienced as a body without organs – a place where the experience of the unknown can advance so that everything becomes insubstantial, or *intensively substantial* –

It's warm tonight, it rained tonight
The windows are all open wide
Can't see the clock to check the time

Nothing is moving
When You Walk Through Me […]
I almost lose me
It's so confusing
When You Walk Through Me

And also –

Talking in the window as the light fades
I heard my voice break
Just for a moment
Talking by the window as the light fades
I felt the floor change into an ocean
We'll never leave here – never
Let's stay in here forever
And when the streets are quiet
We'll walk out in the silence

(these are from the last two tracks, When You Walk Through Me, and Just for a Moment).

There can very definitely be eerie events when alongside the window, as in the song Dislocation ("The sun was going down one quiet evening / Someone came into the room when I was half asleep / We spoke for a while I couldn't see his face / Later on, when he had gone / I realised I had not asked his name"). And it is both the case that the "quiet men" and the entire space of memories, "envisagings" and photographs is slipped outward toward an indeterminate world: the songs evince other dimensions of the body without organs, and encounters with anomalous, enigmatic figures who appear as existing at a high degree of proximity.

Some of them are crowding closer

some of them live in photographs

And in the next song –

Walking they were walking
Through the rainy days
Looking at all the faces.
But no-one ever noticed them
The Quiet Men

These last two songs – Some of Them and The Quiet Men – have something in common with elements of *No-Man's Land*, and also feel like precursors to the paintings, photographs and anomalous beings of *Sapphire and Steel*. And beyond the images (though not really separate from them), there is the window – the gap alongside the quiet place. *Systems of Romance* overall is that rare thing – an eerie album. And the window is the white wall – or wall of fog – of the second sphere of action.

The album is perhaps left to a great extent un-noticed because there is a disjunction that is likely to be experienced as jarring in the first 6 or 7 songs between sober ultra-oneiric lyrics, and a kind of staccato, charged-up singing (it is punk singing, but with words that are so courageously exploratory and suggestive of trance-states that they are likely to be seen as not fitting with punk's feral mode of being). I have always felt that musically the album only fully takes off in the last three songs, starting from the song Maximum Acceleration (this is not a criticism – it all somehow fits together), and at this point the potentially damping effect of the disjunction is left behind. I now get the insistent impression when I listen to the third-to-last track, Maximum Acceleration – and the entire album, in fact – that I am hearing an emphatic message from someone a bit out beyond ordinary reality who is saying, before the tide turns, that there is a need for the oneiric and abstract visions of lucidity, and for both maximum acceleration and slow motion.

* * *

As I walked along the road to Swinton, where I had worked in the shop, in 1979, I felt that in passing this village I would in a sense be going back to 1978. But simultaneously I felt viscerally that I was seeing the beauty of the area at a higher level of dream-like intensity and clarity than I had before, and I knew that this slipping sideways was the vital thing (and it seemed likely that the differential between the two "worlds" of the past was to some extent a kind of emotive distraction). In wanting to get past Swinton I wasn't really wanting to get to a terrain of the past – I was wanting to reach somewhere where the past would just be one element helping to propel me into the Future.

In the four years after 1979 my mother and I had "revolved" around Ryedale in relation to where we stayed in rented accommodation, but without ever living within it – we were always a few miles away in a much less inspiring terrain with fewer trees, and more agricultural devastation. When I had worked in Swinton we had been living near a village called Rillington in a house with an escarpment of the wolds just behind it to the south, and a view north across a flat expanse of fields. We lived there for nearly two years before living in hotels again for a total of one and a half years, interspersed with three or four month stays, during two successive winters, in holiday cottages that were both in villages on the southern fringe of the lower parts of the North York Moors on the road that runs east to Scarborough from Pickering. At the end we returned to live in a house that was also near Rillington (a badly run-down farm-labourer's cottage for which the rent was £15 a month), and for a second time I went and got a job because my mother's trust-fund resources had temporarily run dry. In retrospect it is obvious that my mother's lack of money was both the result of obstinacy in relation to asking for credit and of her intrinsic slowed-down state in relation to practical tasks. For all of the years of this phase of her life my mother would be wandering around in Yorkshire market towns with a shopping bag which would always have a small case in it, in a plastic bag – a case which I knew contained valuable coins bequeathed to her by her father. It would only be later – when I was at college – that I would acquire the image of my mother with a bag containing half a dozen date scones, some green tomato chutney and £300,000 of antique gold coins. These coins would later be sold at Sotheby's, and this money also would be used for hotel nomadism, although by that time I had long ago ceased to be a companion for my mother's journeys around the island.

In 1983 I started studying French at an evening class at a school in Malton, and it was a girl who I met there who brought about the big change. I had told her I wanted to get to university, and in the spring of 1984 she gave me a clipping from a newspaper which was an advertisement for a residential adult education college in North Wales, offering two-year access courses funded by grants. It seems that at each really difficult threshold of my life I have needed a woman to jolt me awake, or draw me forward. In October of the same year the woman who had helped me across most of the initial thresholds was on the platform at Malton station. My mother was glad for me, but she had tears on her cheeks: we waved to each other until the train curved southward around a bend.

* * *

That night I pitched my tent between some very beautiful, slender beech trees, about two miles along a side road from Hovingham (it was a summer of beech trees – two weeks before, I had seen a hill of spectacular beeches on a derelict 18th century estate in mid-Wales, and later I would go to a beech forest in

Croatia so immense that it covers whole valleys and mountains). The last time I had walked along that road it had been very early January in 1978, during the three or four days we spent in Hovingham, before my first visit to the Black Swan. The memory is of the time just before a threshold-crossing, and leaps to the recollection of being over the far side of the unanticipated threshold– the memory of the first morning at the Black Swan, with snow starting to fall.

But what part of me is it that "harks back" to this beautiful, secure world? Is there a part of me that is yearning far too much for a kind of transcendental cosyness? (the will toward cosyness is evidently an aspect of the control-mind: we should only behave as convalescents when we are convalescing).

Turn perhaps in the other direction – the direction of the Talbot Hotel. But think about the beech trees, and about the sky and the planet – envisage a kind, of warm, calm darkness full of the unknown.

What is the thing that has been forgotten?

It is the inseparably conjoined worlds of stories and sexuality. Conjoined in so many ways, from the stories of the romantic love we yearn toward, to sexual fantasies and the libidinally charged story-worlds of submission to "the will of God."

How do we make sexuality the assisting-force of being in love, rather than love being enslaved all along to sexuality? How do we make our dreamings (very much including our dreaming-up of the future) into the assisting-force of our love for Love-and-Freedom, rather than our love for Love-and-Freedom being enslaved to dreamings that block the way to the Outside?

19

So what *was* taking place at the centre of my experiences, in 1978? And what was the snare that was closing around the rabbit's neck?

* * *

Our most powerful – intense – energy is everything that relates to love, and being *in love*, and everything that relates to sexuality. These are the most momentous channels that connect us to the world.

* * *

At one level what was happening was that I was recurrently on the threshold of falling in love, while simultaneously I was acquiring a deep love for the island of Britain, and for one of its areas in particular. At another level what was taking place was an exploration within the domain of sexuality that had a quality of being under some kind of anomalous "pressure," or even of being a kind of struggle, or contestation (as if I was moving toward the bliss of being in love with women in the face of a closely associated, but separate impulsion that felt concupiscent, lacking in the true, ingenuous joy and delight of love).

In the course of that year we must have travelled around 10,000 miles. There were two visits to Devon, two to Southwest Wales, one or two to the Lake District, two or three to London, and maybe six or seven to Northumberland. In general our stays at hotels were for around a week – only very occasionally for a bit longer (I think my mother did not want to attract attention). We stayed probably five times in total in two different hotels in Ilkley, and maybe six times altogether in three different hotels in

York. We probably stayed twice in Thirsk and twice in Northallerton (towns in the northern part of the vale of York, both around 10 miles from the escarpment of the North York Moors) at hotels that respectively were called the Golden Fleece and the Golden Lion. Sometimes in the middle of summer it was hard for my mother to find rooms, and we would have to stay at places for one or two nights, or occasionally go a long distance to somewhere my mother had not been wanting to visit. There were far more places than I have mentioned at which we stayed more than once during that year.

Before going to sleep at night I would recurrently go over all of the hotels and places, starting from the beginning, seeing all the lines of the journeys spread out across a mental map of Britain (eventually – and probably this was not during the 1978 phase – there came a time when I could no longer remember). Without going a step out of my way – though making allowances for the fact that I was going to Malton and Helmsley – in the four days of my visit to Yorkshire this summer I went past ten hotels at which we stayed.

When the hotel-nomadism "bus" finally stopped we were in a small house – a holiday home – in a straggle of houses, called Stirton, that was three miles from Skipton and five miles from Gargrave.

It was around the middle of November. I remember saying to the woman who owned the house, when we got the key from the nearby farm-house where she lived, that I really loved cold winter weather, and her smilingly saying I was likely to see some of it.

She was obviously right, and in fact the winter that was on the way was no ordinary one. By the time it came to an end, in April, I had been both miserably battered and immensely exhilarated by it.

A day or two after the conversation with the owner a long spell of increasingly severe frosts began. It probably continued for about 10 days (I remember feeling neurotically guilty about the enthusiasm I had expressed for severe winter weather to a woman whose life was primarily about looking after livestock). At the end of the frosts there was snow for a day, and then it turned mild again for a while. But with the gaps that are generally there even in a severe British winter, the weather did in fact continue as it had started. There was a phase in January or February when the frost was so severe that I rode my bicycle on the Leeds-Liverpool canal, and walked across the frozen River Aire (the canal was covered in ice and snow for weeks on end). Combined with the circumstances of the house the winter was also severe enough to give me quite bad and prolonged attacks of what was then called bronchitis. I think it would now be called asthma, but whatever the name I sometimes felt – frighteningly – that I was breathing through a ball of wool that had been lodged in my throat.

The house did not have central heating, and was not well insulated. However, I am now fairly sure that the primary cause of my illness was domestic laziness on the part of myself and my mother. If I had taken all my bedding to a launderette, and kept everything dust-free no doubt I would have been fine.

I remember that there were tensions between my mother and myself, and occasional rows – the situation brought to mind the concept of "cabin fever" (a concept I had learned from *The Shining*, although the thought was that the smallish house surrounded by snow and frost was cabin-like and helping to produce disagreements, rather than it being reminiscent of the Overlook Hotel).

But quite a lot of the time I was on my own because my mother had gone off to stay in a hotel somewhere (whenever my mother had a rented house but still had available funds she was likely to spend something like a quarter of the time off on her own in hotels). And at the weekend I would take the bus to Bradford and go ice-skating. I had learned to skate in New

Zealand (partly on a lake in the Southern Alps) and it was something I loved doing, but this was not my only motivation. On one occasion I succeeded in getting talking to a girl, and we walked back to the bus station together, agreeing to meet there to go skating again the next week. I remember standing yearningly in freezing cold the next week, and the girl not arriving (I think I left a message for her in the frost on a window).

On one return journey that was probably in February (and maybe it was that day when the girl did not arrive) it was snowing very heavily during all of the twenty miles back to Skipton, to the extent that at one point the bus had difficulty getting up a hill. But the first really heavy – road-closing – snowfall that I remember was at some point around the end of December or the beginning of January.

That day we were travelling to York, to stay at the Viking Hotel – a modern, quite expensive hotel in the very centre of the city, alongside the river. I was going because we were planning to speak to my sister in New Zealand. Heavy snow had been forecast, and by the time we set off it had been dark for a while, and the snow had been falling for several hours.

The snow was very heavy, and there was enough wind for it to drift. As far as I can recollect my mother thought about the wisdom of the journey at the point where we were travelling, and the fact it was something of a blizzard had become clear – she had no shortage of courage, but she wasn't foolhardy – and she decided she could do it. She was an ~~very~~ experienced driver, used to driving off-road as well as in snow, and she had winter tyres on the car. Also the last third of the journey was on relatively low-lying ground, without hills.

I remember that as we came to the junction onto the dual-carriageway between Leeds and York – we were twenty miles away, and in the middle of nowhere – there were drifts across the approach, and maybe one car in sight on a road that would normally have been like a motorway. My mother chose her spot

and angle, and speeded up into the drift, and we got through –
but I suspect we came close to getting stuck. After that the odds
were probably in our favour, assuming the snow or the wind did
not increase – given that there were still snow-ploughs out on the
road, and occasional cars. Having traversed a huge length of
snow-swept road, with plumes of snow blowing off the edge of
cut drifts (I think eventually we got behind a snow-plough) we
arrived in York. The people at the hotel reception were
impressed – they had been told hours before that the road on
which we had arrived was blocked.

* * *

The Viking Hotel is in the very centre of the city (within the
medieval city walls), right alongside the River Ouse, on its
western bank. It is a wide, unadorned eight-story block, that is
incongruously just a hundred yards downstream from a
medieval guildhall building on the far bank.

One night, in my room at the hotel, a new event occurred in
my explorations of the virtual-real.

I found myself fantasising that I was a teenage girl being
seduced a by a woman who was maybe 10 years older than her.
This fantasy created another ultra-erotic state of sexual bliss, like
the one six months before.

In the years immediately afterwards those two ultra-orgasmic
states – in Wetherby, and then in York – would stand out from
my sexual experience like two mountains I had climbed. But
although in terms of intensity they seemed equivalent, in terms
of their impact upon me there was a subtle but powerful
difference – I was much more *heartened* by the experience at the
Viking Hotel.

And this fact is connected to an intrinsic difference. In the
first experience I had remained in my normal body, but in the
second one I had become a woman. I had taken advantage of

being in a more "fluid" dimension of the body without organs, and I had reached an experience of having the body and way-of-being of an intelligent, sensual girl, aged around 16 (I was 16 myself at the time). And I was more strengthened by what had happened than by the earlier event because this development fitted with my intense feeling about who or what I was – it fitted with my heartfelt perception that I loved women. It is only a matter of time, after that, before the idea begins to appear that you can love women so much you can start to also have dreaming/fantasy experiences of *being* virtual-real women rather than just fantasising about being *with* them. This was further heightened by it being the case that the person with whom I had been making love had also been a woman. It never really bothered me that at some level I might be a repressed lesbian (and given I yearned so much to make love with a woman as a man, it never occurred to me at any stage that I should undergo a sex-change in order to be a lesbian): in fact it intuitively seemed to make sense. If I loved women so much, then how could I *not* at some level be a repressed lesbian?

What were the characteristics of the woman who was seducing me in this experience? She was poised, intelligent, warm (in a distant, subtle way), undemonstratively playful, attractive, and very sensual. But her most foregrounded charac-teristic was that she was skilled at manoeuvring and tricking toward a sexual situation without ever allowing the illusion of disinterest to be broken. In other words, she was chilly in her intense warmth: *there was far more of the delight of power about her than the delight of love.* And I would say that most specifically there was no quality of being *in love* about her, or of a yearning either for me to be in love, or her. This was the female being who in the world of the body without organs taught me that I was capable of becomings. A somewhat eerie presence perhaps.

After that second ultra-intense sexual event everything was much better. The remembered view from this summit was far more heartening – energising - and it functioned to remove any tendency to be perturbed by the memory of the earlier experience (though this ~~this~~ last difference was all really at the level of vulnerability to neurosis).

The vital thing in fact was that I had been given an inchoate but unforgettable awareness of a seventh intent-current: becomings. In a world of the body without organs I had focused myself as a new form – as a young woman.

* * *

After two more months in the holiday cottage we set off again. It was the beginning of March. It would turn out that the winter was not over, but at the time when we returned to "the road" the weather was not wintry – there was no snow on the ground any more, and I think it was relatively mild.

After staying for a few days in Grassington, in Upper Wharfedale, we went up to Hexham, in Northumberland.

We had stayed in Hexham at least twice already. Once in mid-December of 1977, when we had stayed at a hotel called the Beaumont. And once in the summer, when I had cycled there from Northallerton in Yorkshire, and we had stayed in a less expensive hotel, called The Royal. It was the Royal at which we stayed for this third visit.

The hotel was a pleasant, unpretentious place that faced south on the main shopping street, around a hundred yards away from a small market-town department store called Robbs.

I liked Hexham. There was a bright, cheerful quality about the town, and even though there was nothing very charismatic either about the buildings or the location (it is on a sort of low, flattish hill-promontory that extends north into a wide region of the Tyne valley, with green but unspectacular hills in the distance, beyond the river), I had always felt a real affection for it. It had good shops, and some streets with quietly beautiful buildings. I had enjoyed the visit to the town in 1977, and had been having a great time cycling between hotels the second time we were there, so the associations were also very positive.

Some day not long after we arrived I was in the quite large book section of Robbs (the department stores at that time all seemed to sell books). It rained through most of the first part of that day, and sometimes the rain was very heavy. I'm fairly sure that heavy snow had been forecast for the evening, and my memory is that I kept leaving the book department to look out the front door to see if the rain was turning to sleet.

Since I had been around 12, in New Zealand, my habit had been to read entire books in bookshops, and to only ever buy the books I really loved. For some reason I never felt in the least embarrassed while I was doing this – I think I felt that people would always see it as a good thing that an adolescent male was absorbed in a book (I almost never thought about it, although I was careful not be conspicuous – after all, I would have argued, if the book was good enough, I would buy it, and I wasn't destroying it…).

I had read a large number of books in the previous 15 months, but I had bought very few. I had bought *The Shining*, which had been in a rotating book-stand in the foyer of The Talbot Hotel. I had bought *Watership Down*, from the well-stocked bookshop – Hoppers – in Malton's market square. I had bought *Imperial Earth* from the Black Swan. At a hotel on a main road a few miles south of Middlesborough I had also bought *The Fury* – a book which is a part of an emergence of a simultaneous naturalising and feminising of the horror genre that also included *The Shining*, Butler's *Patternmaster* novels, Strieber's *The Hunger*, and *Sapphire and Steel*.

But the book I was reading in Robbs belonged to the genre of the bright/dark transcendental, a genre which is heretical within blocked modernism (it is acceptable to write about the unknown that is monstrous, but it is not at all acceptable to write about the "bright" or "numinous" unknown). The book was *Lord Foul's Bane* – the first book of the Stephen Donaldson trilogy.

In the summer I had started reading this book in Hoppers, in Malton, but had put it down at some point after reading the description of leprosy in the opening pages. I remember I was disturbed, in a hypochondriac way, by the thought of the insidiousness of the leprosy virus – which sets people up, in wiping out the nerve-endings, to destroy themselves through their own negligence. In the previous two months, I had read a bit more in a department store in Bradford – perhaps another 10 pages. I think at this point I stopped because of the vastness and disturbing aspects of the world that was arriving. But I think I also stopped because of something slightly florid and melodramatic that is briefly in effect in the book's opening sequence of events.

This time, in Hexham, I kept reading. I'm fairly sure that within a few chapters I knew I was going to buy the book, despite its awkward aspects (it is the second book that is the really great achievement), but I stayed in the bookshop, enjoying the double drama of the book and the visits to the door of the shop to look at what was happening outside. As the afternoon went on the rain became snow.

I bought the book, went and had dinner in the hotel with my mother, and later I continued reading in my room. Outside the snow was falling, coming on an easterly wind, and it was settling.

It snowed for most of the next three days, alternating between phases of light snow, and long phases of thick snowfall: there was also a strong wind, which meant the snow drifted. Given I was in love with snow, this was the event for which I had been waiting (and it was in fact a very rare occurrence – since then I have never seen a blizzard anything like as intense and prolonged as that one).

The morning after it began I went and bought the next two

books, *The Illearth War*, and *The Power that Preserves*. During that day of the snowstorm and the next – reading very late on what would be three successive nights – I read both of these books, reaching the end of the trilogy at around three in the morning of the second night (the third night of the blizzard, and the third night of reading). By that time every road out of Hexham had been blocked for at least a day – the town was completely cut off, and there were fifteen-foot snowdrifts everywhere in the open areas around the town (you probably have to see a snowdrift on this scale for the words to become meaningful).

And on the third day of reading I discovered I was in the domain of a new coincidence, equivalent to reading *The Shining* while staying in a hotel. When Thomas Covenant leaves behind the ordinary world for the third time he finds that the Land is in the grip of a "preternatural winter". The Land's enemy, the Despiser, has found a way to impose an unceasing, fiercely cold wind – bringing a continual winter of frost and blizzards. During the first half of the book the events take place within a world of severe, blizzard-scoured desolation, and as I lived these events I was also continually going to the window to see the winter storm sweeping through the streets of Hexham.

I loved snow too much for the snowstorm to acquire any association of malevolence. I reached the end of the third book at two in the morning, and I remember looking out at the snow falling – now less heavily, but still being blown by a strong wind – and feeling a kind of serene joy. However, the snow was only one of two sources of this state. The trilogy ends with Covenant in a hospital bed in the ordinary world, in a state of recovery after a life-threatening collapse. He is still a leper; he is still cut off from his wife and his child; the woman who he had loved in the other world is dead. But the end of the book is Covenant smiling for a moment at an empty hospital room – "He smiled because he was alive" (the last sentence). And an answering affirmation came from me in part through the power of this ending to put everything into perspective: an awareness of the joy of being alive was combined with – and woken by – the feeling that in comparison with all of that, I had no problems at all.

The next day I walked up into the hills that rise up from the town to the south. There were now long spells of light snow, with only occasional heavy showers – but the wind remained quite strong, and was still a cold easterly.

Having walked past drifts as high as houses on the way to the top of the hill I reached a place where the snow-ploughs had given up, and where drifts covered the road. I turned onto the windward side of the hill, where the snow had been blown off the fields, and set out walking. The journey was now entirely shaped by the need to stay in the wind, given that anywhere else there were gigantic snowdrifts (with difficulty I crossed one area of woodland, which was full of high drifts even though it was on the exposed side of the hill). To my left was a world of wind and snow sweeping toward me (for a while the snow became quite heavy again).

It was what I had been dreaming about all along. I had reached a place where the human terrain-world had been pre-eminently taken over by the planet. And of course this was a view toward what, at the deepest level, is true all the time. The planet is always pre-eminently the steering or guiding instance in relation to human beings (it is only delusion and fear and arrogance that prevents us from seeing this; and the control-mind destroys us rather than guiding us), with the necessary immediate proviso that the planet itself is in the sway of its own immanent, transecting Outside.

* * *

I think the snow started to thaw the next day. It had never been likely that it would stay for long – it was late March. The blizzard had taken place across the weekend when the clocks were put forward.

After Hexham we travelled to Helmsley, to stay for a week at the Black Swan. I had a room overlooking the market place. And while I was there I re-read the whole of Donaldson's trilogy.

It was the best abstract-oneiric world that I had found. For the next two or three years these books were a primary inspiring force behind the eerie other-world wildernesses and imagined characters that came to my mind when I attempted to write stories. It was as if a gap had been opened in my mind in the direction of the planet, and also in the direction of women as explorers of the unknown. I was haunted by Elena – by this very brief virtual-real incursion from the Future.

With abstract-oneiric systems (dreamings which inspire people to the point of having a guiding impact on their lives) it is only insofar as women are involved within the dreaming as explorers of the unknown that the system is at the level of the real. Otherwise they are obfuscations of the real – they are blocking modalities preventing movement toward the Future, the Outside.

On a few occasions I fantasised about making love with Elena. But although these experiences were intensely erotic, I was always ultimately left with a feeling of having failed (not through shared sensual/sexual bliss, but through the ejaculatory *fucking* at the very end of the dreamed sexual act) to enact and embody the state of being *in love* with the woman about whom I was dreaming. As if there was a quality of *imposition*, and of falling short of what was needed for the true journey.

The gothic aspect of what is eerie about sexuality concerns imposition, and it also concerns damaging surrender of will, or being "imposed upon". And the gothic aspect of what is eerie about stories again concerns imposition (people tend generally to recognise this in relation to the stories created by L. Ron Hubbard etc. but they tend to have a blind-spot – created by an imposition – in relation to the story-worlds of the older religions).

* * *

Late March, 1979. Bob Dylan is now a Christian. In New York Burroughs is back on heroin, and John Lennon has only 18 months left to live. All around Britain there are the first billboard posters for a political party ("Labour isn't Working"). In around a month Margaret Thatcher will be quoting Francis of Assisi on the steps of 10, Downing St.

But in the worlds of the virtual-real I had encountered Elena, and I had woken my becoming-woman not just to the point of sensuality and sexuality, but to the point where I was dreaming of being in love with women who are fearless travellers into the unknown (the Future, the bright-transcendental).

The rabbit had got a paw into the snare.

20

I wrote this prose-poem in the summer of 2006, when I was in a small town in northern Mongolia: I wrote it after having a dream where I was reciting the beginning of it (I think in the dream it had been written by someone else) to a group of people. The era in which the story was set was relatively clear – the event was taking place at some time in the middle of the medieval period, somewhere around the 1200s or 1300s. I think that in the dream there was a stronger quality of the archaic about the language, although it should be added that I was reciting it at the current time (in an ordinary room in a house somewhere in Britain).

Travelled at the falling of the year, westward from London, through winding lanes and mist. The berries of the dog-rose smoldering like old blood. Travelled without hope, with echoes of laughter.

Travelled at the falling of the year, where the walls between the worlds grow thin, she said. Echoes of laughter, at the falling of the year.

Priest and crusader, and theologian-philosopher, defeated at last by a woman from beyond the dyke of Offa, by a woman and two men, all from beyond the boundaries of my thought.

The white horse, ancient chalk message from the future, three hundred feet broad, travelling upwards, south by southwest.

The man who greeted me, as if by chance, living in a cottage beneath the chalk rise, five leagues from the horse – the man who greeted me, outwarden of the impossible.

Over three days played many old games of skill and thought. Sometimes I won, and often ran him close, but most often he triumphed with unreadable quietness, with disarming grace.

He said, I know her you seek, she has passed through, and said you might come this way, at the falling of the year.

Snow across the vale, bright and deep, an expanse westward, speaking to me of high western hills, and futures alive in deep valleys.

Snow on the white horse, white upon white, the horse of the mind lying blanketed with snow.

Time to skirt the sun's path, time to travel westward, at the rising of the year.

* * *

Looked at from the perspective of the dreamings with which it is connected – the perspective of the "oneirosphere" – what is the area of hills centred on the valley of the river Rye?

It can be said immediately that the chalk white horse in the Hambleton Hills – on an escarpment eight miles from Helmsley – is a link to the White Horse of Uffington, a hill-figure which is around 2700 years old. The "Kilburn white horse'" is one of the very few white horse hill-figures outside of the Wiltshire/ Oxfordshire Downs: in common with all of the others apart from the initial one it is not ancient – it was made in 1857, at the top of an escarpment looking out over the village of Kilburn, and over the Vale of York (it is visible from forty miles away). This hill figure is almost entirely surrounded by trees – it seems to have more trees around it than any other.

The Kilburn white horse, through the connection to the one above the village of Uffington, is one feature within Ryedale that contributes to the area having its own "eerie arcadianism"; or "eerie ancientism". The two classical "temples" built by the Duncombe family in the eighteenth century, in woodland at the top of the hill above the ruins of Rievaulx Abbey, are very much another element. And so are the ground-level foundations of Hawksmoor's Temple of Venus (strikingly, this was never rebuilt after it collapsed in the 1940s) and the still-existing Temple of the Four Winds (originally the Temple of Diana), both on hill-tops in the grounds of Castle Howard. But the primary source of this affect is the fact that the rolling and often woodland-covered hills that stretch south from the white horse have an idyllic English-arcadian quality (they could be in Oxfordshire, or Devon, or Warwickshire...), and yet, despite this quality they are not connected to any dreaming created in the area. There is no connection to the Brontes, for instance, and nor is there any connection to the romantic poets, or to other poets or writers who have created dreamings out of their terrains (as with Housman in Shropshire, or Hardy in "Wessex"). Given the arcadian-idyllic beauty of the area, and given that it is in England, this vacuum can only be filled by Shakespeare (and by the other writers who are naturally alongside Shakespeare, and closely associated with him, such as Woolf, and Dunsany).

It should be said at this point that Laurence Sterne lived in a village a few miles south of the Kilburn white horse. But *Tristram Shandy* is not a dreaming about the area where it was written. During the entire time I lived in and around Ryedale I encountered – so far as I remember – no reference to Sterne as a local figure. I read *Tristram Shandy* because I heard it dramatized on the radio, and even though I read it when I was living near Malton I don't remembering making the connection. But this is because the book is primarily critique: it is not at all haunted by a place – instead it is haunted by human affectations and opinions. The terrain of the book is a sketched backdrop for the impressively – and revealingly – bizarre characters, and it is the bare minimum necessary to maintain the power of a dreaming for a book which consists more of subtle observations than of described events. I experienced *Tristram Shandy* as taking place in an indeterminate terrain somewhere in 18th century England – a terrain whose details were in no way important in the book's world.

Malton and Helmsley therefore show no tendency to see themselves as doorways to "Tristram Shandy country". This phrase destroys itself immediately, precisely because the book consists primarily of satire.

It is also the case that they are not able to present themselves as doorways to "Brideshead Revisited country." Although Castle Howard has been the set for two adaptations, the house in the novel is in Wiltshire. The world of dreamings is of course in no way affected by the constraints of tourist marketing, but in any case the vital elements of the Brideshead Revisited world revolve as much around Oxford as they do around Brideshead.

What people tend to remember about the adaptations of the novel is a "golden age" affect of Oxford (and the country around it) in the 1920s or 1930s, which of course is the high-point of the first phase of the newly emergent world of modernism. The novel in its opening pages faintly makes the connection to the new modernist tradition of "strange tales" – which had started in Oxford – by talking about the "low door in the wall" that can be found in the city, leading to a somewhere-else, an "enchanted garden" (and its connection to modernism's "eerie ancientism" is made by the title of this first chapter – "et in arcadia ego"). So Brideshead Revisited is not really a strong presence in relation to Ryedale (again, when the series was shown in 1982 I have no memory of discovering that the "stately home" in the series was Castle Howard), and insofar as it *is* a presence it seems to mostly open up a kind of oneiric continuity of English arcadian places, one which can only have Shakespeare's dreamings as its pre-eminent world, especially given that Shakespeare created a conti-nuity of forests between Arden (in Warwickshire, very close to Oxford), Ardennes in France, and Arcadia in Greece.

* * *

To complete this overview it is necessary to tell the story of the combined social and religio-oneiric worlds of the "estab-lishment" of the area. This is a story of three defeats that deeply fracture the region's control-mind oneiric force-field (and leave it somewhat in abeyance, so that overall the area is a little more open to the planet, the Future – Love-and-Freedom). It is also the story of a turning of a tide – of a moment when the down-trodden west of the island at last spoke back against an entrenched colonial imposition.

* * *

The lake in the vale of Pickering had gone. Before the Romans arrived there were the Celtic or Brittonic people who belonged to the same family of peoples whose social world in "Oxfordshire" created the white horse on the hill above Uffington. For these people both men and women could be views toward the sacred, in that in some sense they believed in both goddesses and gods (male and female non-human, ultra-human or trans-human spirits). After the Romans had come and gone, the Norsemen had arrived, and had created the "Danelaw", a large kingdom (including Gloucestershire, Oxfordshire, and Northumberland), that had York, or Yorvik, as its capital city. The area was now pre-eminently split between the Norse oneiric systems (and whatever remained of the Brittonic and Anglo Saxon dreamings) and the Christian system – which had a connection to York, because of the fact that the man who became the first Christian emperor,

Constantine, was proclaimed emperor in the city, in AD306.

York was the centre of the largest kingdom of the island because it was in the middle of one the biggest areas of fertile arable land, and also because this time the colonial power had come from the northeast, rather than the south.

The first defeat for the area was a twofold process. The event that would lay waste to the area, and totally transform its social fabric, was not the vanquishing of the Danelaw's army by Harold, but the subsequent cataclysmic defeat – and massacre – visited upon it by the new colonial power, the Normans.

Yorkshire was the primary target of this slaughter – which maybe involved the deaths of 100,000 people across all of the areas that were attacked.. The events took place in the winter of 1069-1070, and the aim was the prevention of rebellions in an area that might ally itself with a Danish invasion force. In what became known as "the harrowing of the North" the soldiers of William the Conqueror attacked villages across the region, killing their inhabitants, and destroying their livestock and supplies of food. By all accounts the famine that followed led to a very large number of deaths. In 1086 the Domesday Book entries record extreme devastation in a ~~very~~ large number of Yorkshire estates.[32]

After this event the vale of Pickering was surrounded by a ring of castles (at Malton, Pickering, Helmsley and Scarborough). And very soon the monasteries were established – monasteries which are generally regarded as having been an agent of colonialism, in a situation where the governing aristocracy remained for centuries separate from the governed population. Rievaulx was founded early, in 1132 (and went on to become one of the largest and most successful in Yorkshire), and Byland Abbey, 8 miles away, was founded a few years later. The Norman "yoke" in the area consisted of castles, and of French-speaking monks threatening people with eternal torture by demons if they stepped out of line, and was of course given a powerful "glamour" by some impressive gothic architecture.

All of this had York Minster at its centre, a gigantic gothic cathedral, built out of whitish-yellow sandstone, standing out floatingly from the wide plain, despite its immense bulk. The signs on the road from Helmsley to Rievaulx refer to the remains of the abbey as an "ancient monument", but this name somehow serves to obscure the fact that the ruined abbeys in the area were close cousins of the celebrated building in York, built at exactly the same time.

But the abbeys were not simply ecclesiastical. They were top-of-the-system landowners and employers, owning and running not only huge areas of farms, but other ventures as well. Rievaulx Abbey had a profitable iron mine further up the valley, which had had an extremely efficient furnace – apparently an early, rare example of the blast furnace.

* * *

At the time of the second defeat for the area Helmsley Castle was owned by Richard the Third, the king who belonged to the "house of York". But the west that began to speak back with the defeat of Richard was ultimately Wales, rather than Lancashire. This new defeat for Yorkshire was visited upon it by Henry Tudor: Henry was the grandson of Owain ap Maredudd ap Tudur, and Owain was the man who as a squire (with his name modified to Owen Tudor) at the court of Catherine de Valois widow of Henry the Fifth, had formed an initially secret relationship with Catherine. Owain's father – going back one more generation – had lost almost all his lands as a result of supporting Owen Glendower's rebellion against English rule, so the family had opposition to the world of Norman power in its very recent past.

The defeat of Richard the Third at Bosworth was the initial

event that set up the major development a generation later. Again, it is a two-stage process – and this time the second stage is what is called "the dissolution of the monasteries" (although Bosworth was the point where the Yorkist faction was defeated, it was the later event that would transform and fracture the social fabric of Ryedale). But all of this notwithstanding, the more important issue is that this fight-back of the west is really just a precursor of something far more extraordinary that would happen during the *second* generation after Henry Tudor's victory and twenty five year reign – the arrival of the dreamings of Shakespeare.

* * *

Three hundred years earlier there had been another precursor, and one that intrinsically involved both the oneirosphere, and an explicit evincing of the body without organs – *The History of the Kings of Britain* (published in 1137). But despite the fact that Geoffrey of Monmouth's creation of the Arthurian mythos – together with its subsequent elaborations – would end up playing quite an important socio-political role, this also was very much only a faint indicator of what was possible.

In Geoffrey's tale everything turns around Uther wanting to have sex with a woman so intensely that he uses the anomalous knowledge of Merlin to make it happen (Arthur is the result of an adulterous act where his mother was not guilty of a betrayal because she believed she was having sex with her husband). [33] In the case of Henry the Eighth - inheritor of his father's Tudor victory at Bosworth – it is Henry's divorce and remarriage, in the face of a refusal of papal permission, that constitutes the split from Catholicism that in turn leads to the transformation of Ryedale. The complete sweeping away of all the monastic foundations – and the making uninhabitable of the abbey buildings – was a gigantic change for the area, given the power and prestige of both Rievaulx and Old Byland.

The lines that run between the arrival of the Tudor dynasty at Bosworth and the destruction of the monasteries are not easy to trace. Whatever might have happened without the Tudors (it seems that no matter what took place monastic power was close to a major diminishment), all that can be said is that for Yorkshire there was a military defeat followed a generation later by a defeat of a different kind. In 1536 there was a huge popular uprising in defence of the monasteries which succeeded in taking the city of York, and re-instating Catholicism there. 30,000 people marched on Doncaster in what was called "the pilgrimage of grace", but the uprising was defused with a series of false promises, and then the leaders were arrested, and more than 200 of them were charged with treason and executed.

The monasteries had been flagship symbols of Norman power and "sophistication," and as agents of colonialism they had been vital in the process of entrenchment of the French-speaking aristocracy onto England and Wales. But although the second Tudor monarch was a Norman born in London he was also from the west by affiliation through his father. And the west had endured a great deal. It had been defeated by the Romans, and had been submitted to colonisation from Rome for centuries. And then it had endured four hundred years of colonial domination from the Normans (and the monasteries for those resisting the colonisation would have been the most insidious and disturbing aspect of the imposition, because of their supposed "innocence" in the colonisation). But unlike in Yorkshire, where the "harrowing of the north" simply swept away most traditions that could have maintained resistance, in Wales a culture, a language, and an indigenous world of rebellious influential families had maintained itself. Henry was an inheritor of this tradition – and it should be added that he could not have succeeded if for the overall population (ignoring those aristocrats who were going to be given the lands) there had not been many for whom the "unthinkable" was decidedly thinkable all along. It is very obviously the case that Henry the Eighth was the opposite of a hero – he was a Bluebeard-like figure whose degree of power meant he required no unvisited room for his atrocities – but it needs to be seen that he was drawing on an oneirically powerful legitimation-system. In *The History of the Kings of Britain* (regarded at the time as factual) Arthur is a Celtic king, from what would later be Wales, who goes to war on the continent with the Roman legions and defeats them, and who only stops in his march on the city of Rome (effectively already vanquished) because he is called back to Britain. "Rome" had a – supposedly – very different meaning in the time to which these events were attributed, but for those looking on at the split from Catholicism the impact of this story would recurrently have been the thought that Britain should not be ruled in *any* sense by Rome.

* * *

(It should be said at this point that all of this is primarily about what can be called the "ecumenon" – the world of the power formations of the human socio-religious household.[34] And there is *always* war in the ecumenon.)

* * *

In Ryedale the consequence of the socio-religious shift was that the aristocracy of the area were now split. The most powerful and prestigious family in the area were the Howards (relatives of the Dukes of Norfolk), and they became a "recusant" family, refusing to give up their catholicism. This has not changed: a fact given indirect emphasis by the TV and film versions of Brideshead Revisited (which despite its connection to modernism is an intrinsically catholic novel) both having used Castle Howard as a set, and by the fact that what is perhaps

England's pre-eminent Catholic public school – the two-hundred-year-old Ampleforth College, with its Abbey – is located a few miles to the north of the estate.

The resulting situation was one where it was simply not possible for anyone to take a locally undisputed position with respect to the fundamental stances of the socio-religious world. The aristocrats of Castle Howard did not in any final sense accept the authority in religious matters of the archbishop of York twenty miles away – the household of religious dreaming in the area could not be set in order. And in these circumstances a process of keeping the blocked-oneiric aspect of the ecumenon in abeyance seems to have been the response. Confronted by the beguiling "splendour" of an aristocratic family if you ask people to feel their way into a sense of what is wrong with catholicism they might just end up feeling that the same problems are present in anglicanism (the two religions are extremely similar).

The overall shift at this time was evidently one that went far beyond the domain of the ecumenon. It culminated in the emergence of free, unfettered dreamings , and their immediate emplacement at the centre of the social field. And it reached the point where the oneirosphere was productively in effect within politics in a way that was linked to the worlds of the un-blocked dreamings.

Uther's illicit sexual relationship with Igraine led to Arthur. Henry's illicit relationship with Anne Boleyn (illicit from the point of view of the previous moral code of the country, and of Catholicism) led not to a male heir, but to Elizabeth. A kind of "golden age" was indeed about to happen, but it was going to have a vector of becoming-woman at its centre (and not just at the centre of politics, but at the centre of religion, in that Elizabeth became head, or Supreme Governor, of the new English Catholicism). Henry was extremely disappointed, and the dominant ecumenal assemblage of the time was about to be given a task of legitimation that by necessity would be open to innovative oneiric means.

With Elizabeth a spectacular change has happened. It is not surprising that when Virginia Woolf goes back in time in time to write her two oneiric-abstract histories of England – *Orlando*, and *A Room of One's Own* – she goes back in both cases to the time of Elizabeth. And it is a generally un-noticed fact that Dunsany's *The King of Elfland's Daughter* (written at around the same time as Woolf's books) also reads like a history of the Elizabethan era, and of what happened in England over the next three hundred years, with the one proviso that in certain ways what happened in the second half of the sixteenth century is far more extraordinary than what takes place in the novel. The start of Dunsany's strange tale is a meeting of a small group of "elders" where it is decided that it would be good if their country - which is called Erl – was ruled by "a magic lord", and that they should set out to make this happen. This has an extraordinary parallel in what happens in Elizabethan England. Initially there is the story of "the Virgin Queen", making Elizabeth into a walking sacred being. But then this is taken immeasurably further by her being characterised as "the *Fairy* Queen."

It can be seen that for the ecumenal power-brokers of the time the situation is very grave. The queen has been declared by the pope to be illegitimate at birth (born out of wedlock) and illegitimate as a sovereign, and the demand has been made that those adhering to the new "anglican" religion come back into Catholicism or face eternal damnation. Elizabeth being represented as a "Virgin Queen" is a vital step in the direction of giving a good foundation-story for the new church (especially given that her semi-psychotic father had brought about the rift with Rome because he wanted to re-marry, rather than for theological, Lutheran reasons). But the fact that she was a woman born into a curse (through being illegitimate from the viewpoint of Rome) dictated that anything would be used to give a glow of the 'transcendental' to her image, including poetry that exalted her by means of allegorical complements, and including outright magical tales. Spenser's *Fairie Queen* is the intermediate step, making possible a very smooth transition. And after that the door is wide open for Shakespeare to create a work involving a Fairy Queen that is not allegorical, but is instead a vital element in an abstract-oneiric beckoning to the Outside consisting of several magical stories at a spectacular level of lightness and power.

Suddenly England does have a magic lord, only it is a woman – it is Elizabeth. And her magic has nothing to do with the monarchy: it has to do with her having an associated form in the oneirosphere, that of "the Fairy Queen".

* * *

It is necessary to see the context for this event, which of course is just an aspect of something far wider, and far more important.

In the Elizabethan era there is a resurgence of both of the fundamental aspects of the world that have been suppressed by control-mind monotheistic systems: the female, and the planet. A lone woman is enough to bring the female to the foreground if she is sovereign and head of the new religious establishment. And the planet had just been opened up as an "object" of fascination because the age of global maritime exploration had begun, and had become a fundamental aspect of the life of England as a nation. Shakespeare took the lightning of the time, and conducted it. And with his Welsh grandmother, and coming from Stratford-on-Avon – *afon* means river in Welsh -Shakespeare is *the* moment where the west at last speaks back.

* * *

However, it is important to see the extent to which the English zone of the ecumenon was on shaky ground with its new positions in relation to Britain and religion. There was a tendency at the highest levels to draw on the post-Geoffrey elaborations of the Arthurian mythos to provide legitimacy for the idea of Anglicanism as the true Catholic church (because "the Holy Grail" was brought to Britain), or to draw on the whole system of stories to invoke the idea of a past golden age of right and righteous conduct that had taken place in Britain and involved a successful struggle against Rome. It was also the case that *The History of the Kings of Britain* (still generally accepted as a work of history) provided a high-kudos foundation-story for the whole country, tracing the lineage of rulers back to Troy. But for anyone intelligently scrutinising the texts it would have been clear that none of this was going to last. Shakespeare was therefore in a society where anyone producing dreamings that could powerfully support the new monarchical and religious establishment would be given an immense amount of latitude.

Shakespeare went back 2500 years to the time of his major predecessor, Sophocles. And he did not do this to write a foundation story or provide support for the current political and religious system: he went there to gain understanding though making contact with the eerie arcadian worlds of the ancient Greeks. And there was a sense in which he never came back – or rather a sense in which this movement at a deeper level was an arrival in the Future. And because of the need for support for the establishment (through reflected glory, through the idea of "the Fairy Queen"), the Future was allowed to speak, and a door was created in the oneirosphere that was located right in the high-energy centre of the social field.

Shakespeare's worlds are initiators toward awareness of the body without organs: in *The Tempest* when a group of spirits he has summoned disappears Prospero says they "have melted into air, thin air", and to point out the strangeness of the physical substance of a human being Shakespeare has Prospero say (a few lines later) "we are such stuff as dreams are made on." When taken together *The Tempest* and *A Midsummer Night's Dream* have a powerful planetary aspect (Puck flies around the planet) and their un-populated – and highly feminine – landscapes are strongly suggestive of the second sphere of action. Furthermore, the anomalous unknown is powerfully opened up as a perspective through the presence of the inorganic beings within these – very eerie - forests and wild expanses (Ariel is an example of one kind of inorganic being, or "spirit," and Puck is another).

* * *

The third defeat in Ryedale was in the Civil War. In Yorkshire there was support for the parliamentarians mainly in the west of the county, where the wool-textiles industry was based, and the rural northern and eastern areas were all royalist. After the victory of the parliamentarians at Marston Moor (which is a few miles outside York) there was a phase of sieges where the Norman castles of the north of the county were held by royalist forces. Helmsley castle was besieged, and when eventually it was taken, it was partially destroyed, by decree, to prevent royalists using it again (this was the pattern all across Yorkshire – the Norman castles were partially dismantled, like the monasteries a century before).

After this defeat Ryedale had achieved the extraordinary result of being a very attractive, atmospheric area which was nonetheless relatively untroubled by local heroic narratives. It had no extant connection to royalty (and the ancient connections were to the disgraced Richard the Third); its major aristocratic family, the Howards, could not straightforwardly "lord it" over the area in relation to religion, because they were Catholics; and it had no local literary or military heroes whose successes had become enshrined as functioning elements of the ecumenon.

And this did not really change. Captain James Cook came

from the northern edge of the North York Moors, well beyond Ryedale, and given that he was an explorer his power as a "territorialising" figure could only be limited. No stultifying system of romance could easily be distilled from Laurence Sterne's tendency to light-heartedly critique everything. And a century later Bram Stoker having Dracula come ashore at Whitby created a gothic literary connection for the eastern wing of the moors, but no gloomy "warning to the curious" gothic mythos attached itself directly to Ryedale's two ruined monasteries.

In the eighteenth century the fending-off of encounters with the unknown began to take place to a greater extent through a constrained form of reason (without assistance of lucidity): classicism was everywhere, but in the form of geometrical gardens, and grandiose architecture, as opposed to eerie arcadias. The system of reason-revelation did not yet start to disable the over-arching discursive power of religion, and the new unfettered dreamings were kept in the background by an ongoing puritanical tendency in religion, and by the locked-down "enlightenment" fixation on critique and formal systems.

Most immediately what was being fended off at this time was Shakespeare – or rather, the focused lucidity in the face of the unknown that now had an exemplar in the world of socially established dreamings. However, it was only a matter of time: the enlightenment was followed by "romanticism." This new movement was still bleakly inflected by the enlightenment, but it returned Shakespeare to the foreground, and, more importantly, it made people open to the possibility *of thinking by means of writing anomalous tales.*

Christina Rossetti's *Goblin Market* is part of the breakthrough. It is followed almost immediately by *Alice in Wonderland* and *Alice Through the Looking Glass.* And then very shortly afterwards there is *Thus Spoke Zarathustra* – and modernism has gone into full effect.

If you walk north from the Kilburn white horse – created in

1857 – you reach Arden Great Moor, which is at the northwest of the hills that are drained by the river Rye. Standing on the escarpment of these hills, and looking northwest, you are looking toward Croft on Tees (fifteen miles away), the village that was Lewis Carroll's home from the age of 11 until he began to live permanently in Oxford.

* * *

In 1991 I met up with my mother in Malton. I was at Warwick University, in the last year of an undergraduate degree. My mother had come down from her house in Sunderland in the north of Scotland (the house was a converted railway station on a line that was still in use).

We stayed at the Talbot Hotel. As if the comrades from the escape had found a way of returning for a moment to a place that had been central to it. It was thirteen years later.

I had *The Logic of Sense* with me, Deleuze's extrapolation of outsights from the dreamings of Lewis Carroll. I remember reading it in the hotel, excited by the parts of it I understood, and getting the false impression I was beginning to bring it all into focus.

* * *

My "dream" experience when I took DMT (and saw the Black Swan Hotel) happened around nine years ago. I was with two friends in a house in north London.

I took it in two stages. First I inhaled a half-dose, to acclimatise myself – to see where I might be going. Then a short while later I took the full amount.

When I inhaled the half-quantity I was immediately seeing a room which had an opening onto a street in a small town (it was as if part of the back wall was missing, and this gave the view down the length of the street). The walls and floor of the room were covered in small, repeating coloured patterns that looked faintly South American, or central American. There was a brightness about everything, but a kind of pale brightness: everything looked very much as if it was a cartoon.

In front of me was a cartoon-man sitting at a table with an open book on it, whose pages consisted of more patterns, like the ones on the walls, although I think they were more intricate. He was a small, stocky, cartoon figure, wearing a sombrero that came down over the top of his face. Instead of eyes there was a black straight line of his hat across his face (a stylised or "cartoon" line). The man was an extraordinary presence, radiating both a sense of humour, and a kind of fierce, poised intensity. It was through looking at the middle section of the line of his sombrero (and of the space underneath it where his eyes would have been, if they had been visible) that everything happened in the experience, beyond the initial situation.

In looking toward the eyes of the figure what was communicated to me with immense power (and my memory is that this took place without words) was the question – "Are you *ready* for this?" The question was very heavily emphasised, but in an impersonal, neutral way, as if it was primarily pointing out the intensity of what was about to happen when I took the full amount of DMT. There was no quality either of mockery or concern in relation to my degree of readiness. The only other aspect was a kind of fierce lightness, or brightness: an amusement that felt abstract, rather than directed at me – as if it was about the difference between how people see the world, and how it really is, and about the general phenomenon of unreadiness for the transition from deluded to clear perception.

The other thing that happened as I looked into the black line of the sombrero (and this took place two or three times) was that I would suddenly be seeing something like a large bonfire at night. As if I was in a clearing of a forest on a very dark night, and I was seeing a blazing bonfire a hundred feet away. This gives the feeling of what I saw, but primarily what I was seeing was a bonfire-like blaze of white flames surrounded by blackness (the light was white, rather than orange)

There was a consistency about it all: after this other view (which was momentary) I would be back seeing the room with the man at the table.

The end of the experience was an extraordinary visual "joke", or playful *tour de force* of perception. A group of cartoon-aliens appeared from either side of my visual field (I think two from each side). They had coloured skin and diversely "mis-shapen" bodies, and they proceeded immediately to use ladders to dismantle the room I had been seeing, as if they were in front and it could it be pulled down in small two-dimensional pieces. As they did this the living room in which I was sitting became visible. It was a kind of joke-performance lasting only a few seconds: having removed everything the cartoon-aliens disappeared to left and right, the way they had come, carrying their ladders, leaving me with an unobstructed view of the living room.

* * *

I inhaled the full quantity about half an hour later. This time the smoke made me cough, and I did not drink enough water before being swept away into the experience (I think it is possible that a lack of full physical composure affected my ability to hold onto memories).

The first event was that I suddenly had three beings right in front of me who had come to take me somewhere (this was what I knew within the experience about their intention). They were exceptionally "insistent" presences that communicated an urgency (or maybe a necessary speed) by being in front of me and pulsing toward me and back again extremely fast, in a kind of ultra-fast pounding of back-and-forward motion that was also the statement "come with us".

They were also "cartoon beings" but at a level which had become abstract. The beings were in the form of coloured rectangular shapes that were like shields – they were oriented vertically, and had different colours: one was green and I think another was yellow. There seemed to be an articulation of the shield half way up, as if the shield was made of two overlapping plates. There was a bright, intelligent "characterfulness" about these beings: each had a personality, but they did not feel at all as if they were human. Two of the beings were female.

I only have two clear memories after this, one located at the end of the experience, and one that is indeterminate in the "span" of what happened. In relation to unclear recollections what I remember is that a vast series of very extraordinary and very positive things happened, and that despite my attempts to hold onto them, they all, with one exception, fell away – were lost from memory.

It had all just been happening: a world of astonishing experiences. And now I was walking – or maybe floating – in a windowless version of the Black Swan Hotel. I was going toward the front of the hotel, the part of the building that faces south. There was a serene atmosphere, an atmosphere of secure, quiet warmth (it felt as if it was in some sense a subterranean place, but at the same time as if there was not really any gravity there – unless you wanted to act as if there was – so the feeling of it being subterranean was counteracted by the feeling of it being in gravity-free space). The quality of the illumination was that of electric light (the way the hotel would be at night). And there was no impression at all that what I was seeing was like a cartoon.

As I was reaching the end of the corridor the experience ended, and I was back in the living room. Only it had not quite ended – I had managed to hold onto a memory from earlier, and under these circumstances to remember can be to re-experience , to re-live the event. I remembered that I had been shown (by the beings within the experience that had just take place) the depth-level nature of the world in relation to energy, feeling and intent. And this had been done by means of a kind of "fan-spectrum" coloured diagram, whose lines and colours started out as vertical on the left, and then dropped down – through ninety degrees – to horizontal, on the right. On the left, at the vertical, was love, which I think was a white-violet colour. And on the right, at the horizontal, was control or domination – and this was black. In between there was a graduated world of states of energy, feeling and intent that was on a spectrum between the vertical and the horizontal.

The experience I remembered did not have any other details (I was shown the diagram by it being in front of me – there is no memory of a visible presence of the beings who were showing it to me). But the memory is not at all cartoon-like: which is not just to say that there was a warmth and depth to the colours – the experience at this point was of being *within* a space, rather than seeing things on a "screen" in front of me. And the place where it happened was a room-like space within a large, sequestered, "warmly secure" world (without windows, but also without gravity) – a world belonging to the beings who had "come to get me" at the start of the experience. It should at this point be added that my impression with all of the events that I do not remember was very much that they had all taken place in this world (and it has always felt that there was a total continuity in the transition to the experience of being in the Black Swan Hotel – and that at this point I was still in the place, but was being shown the "fabric" of the place itself, by means of something familiar to me).

The re-living of the experience of seeing the diagram culminated in something new. The beings who had shown it to me now "told" me something (though I don't remember words being used) which had the quality or form of a joke. It was pointed out to me that human beings – and this very much included me – had in front of them all the time the fact that the world really consists of energy, feeling and intent, but that they obdurately, stupidly – and pretentiously – cling to their opinion that the world is a dull, ordinary, "concrete" place. The joke in the end was very much on me – directed brightly toward me. I laughed, and there was a real joy in the laughter (I felt I had not laughed like that for ten years, or more). I went into the world of the "inorganic beings" coughing, and I came back with the cough transformed into laughter.

* * *

However, it remains the case that I was not really overwhelmed – apart from in the moment of laughter – by the insight about the depth-level nature of the world: this was because I already viewed the world in this way (helped initially by Spinoza, and in particular by Deleuze, with his concept of the body without organs). It is pointed out in Castaneda's books that inorganic beings (whether they are consistent phenomenological elements within human awareness, or independent entities living in a neighbouring dimension) have a tendency to tell people what they know already. This seems to be exemplified by my DMT experience, though it is true both that the concise, diagrammatic way in which I was shown the "outsight" was new and impressive, and that through the joke levelled against me I received a powerfully emphasised reminder that I needed to embody my knowledge.

* * *

The enlightenment was a fear of the unknown. Despite the fine-tuning of reason involved, it was all along a darkening, simply because there was a shutting down of vital parts of what had been used to see the world (the enlightenment discarded dreamings, along with fallacious religious reasoning, and in the process suppressed lucidity).

Kubrick was haunted by the shiny, desperate bleakness of the enlightenment. At the end of *2001; A Space Odyssey* the astronaut sees space-age enlightenment interiors which are associated with degenerative age. And his next film, *Barry Lyndon* (partly filmed at Castle Howard), is entirely set in a denuded, debased 18th century world, whose "glamour" has been emptied of dreamings that are expressions of love and lucidity. Just before the enlightenment the era of maximal attacks on village wise women (and other female travellers into the unknown, in general) occurred across Europe: many thousands of women were tortured and killed. On one level (the level of the functioning of the system of revelation-reason) the enlightenment was a second phase in a crushing of women's' openness to the unknown (Shakespeare, with his magic, and his extraordinary female characters, had got out of hand – opening a pathway to Love-and-Freedom). The first phase is a representing of sorceresses and female shaman figures as evil, and a process of "showing" – by means of brutal murders – that they will meet a horrific end. The second phase (and this one is directed at reason, as opposed to a semi-awake lucidity) is to convince everyone that they do not exist.

When modernism goes into full effect it is suffused with a becoming-woman, and with spaces that are intensely suggestive of the second sphere of action. It is a very extraordinary incursion of the Outside.

Before long there will be the focused lucidity of Virginia Woolf, and the metamorphosis of *Orlando*, who becomes a woman at some point in the late seventeenth century. But at the very beginning there is Christina Rossetti, and the empty and eerie landscape of the two sisters who live and sleep together, without a man in the household, and have to stave off something deeply and fatally twisted in the libidinal world (Rosetti said – of course – that she wrote *Goblin Market* as a poem for adults). Then there are the *Alice* books (whose structuring games are outside the semiotic field of Christianity, chess having been invented in India, and playing cards in China), followed not long after by *Thus Spoke Zarathustra*, which in turn is followed by Carroll's *Sylvie and Bruno*, a world which momentarily includes a mysterious professor, who is called Mein Herr, and who comes from another planet.

* * *

Thus Spoke Zarathustra is philosophy crossing the threshold into dreaming. Nietzsche earlier had started out – as with Shakespeare – going to Ancient Greece, but here he goes to Ancient Iran, around 3000 years ago. However the world inhabited by Zarathustra is in Nietzsche's own time – it is just that it is a world that is off to the side of the present. A place of wildernesses in which there are only occasional, wandering individuals (who are explicitly contemporary, as opposed to anciently historical, while at the same time being "un-timely", transhistorical). It is a seeing of the second sphere of action, with its extraordinary foregrounding of animals, its planetary emphasis (particularly the love of the planet's sky), and the transcendental importance it gives to the female – the feminine.

For Nietzsche life is a woman, the sky is a woman ("do you not have the sister-soul of my insight?"[35]), and *eternity* is a woman:

Never yet did I find the woman by whom I wanted children, unless it be this woman, whom I love: for I love you, O Eternity![36]

And it is also extremely clear that Nietzsche sees what he calls his soul – which is the part of him which is lucid and creative –

as female: "O my soul, now you stand superabundant and heavy [...] expectant [...] and yet embarrassed because of your expectancy [...]" ( ).Two pages later he takes up the thought again, saying, "Blessed is he who is thus pregnant!"[37]

Nietzsche still has a reason-obsession distortion in his thought due to not having got entirely clear of a fixation on the line of time (the line of time had become more-than-normally foregrounded in the 19th century, because of Darwin, Hegel, etc, but a fixation on it is always a feature of the constricted form of reason). Tying it into a ring ("the ring of recurrence," as he calls it – the envisaged cycle of eventual exact cosmic repetition) evidently does not solve his time-fixation problem at all. But then in the culminating section, called Midday, he lets go at last of the interposed dysfunctional line in relation to eternity – which he sees explicitly as female – and sees eternity through the optic of the sky, re-affirming in the process his femaleness in relation to the body without organs:

O sky above me (he said, sighing, and sat upright), are you watching me? Are you listening to my strange soul?

When will you drink this drop of dew that has fallen on all earthly things – when will you drink this strange soul -

when, well of eternity! Serene and terrible noontide-abyss, when will you drink my soul back into yourself?[38]

(Midday is the fundamental moment in both *Thus Spoke Zarathustra* and *Picnic at Hanging Rock*).

Apart from *Thus Spoke Zarathustra* Nietzsche's work is in many ways a kind of chaotic building site. There are many finished things – passages of sustained lucidity – but overall there is a persistent incompleteness, together with an overall tendency to be a fixated and sometimes un-focused practitioner of critique (this fixation on critique is in some ways similar to that of Laurence Sterne, an author Nietzsche liked).

Nietszche knows he is up against "gravity". He attacks the world of self-importance, damaging moral judgements, resentment, bad conscience (etc) and is very much free of this world, in a way that is reminiscent of the impersonal quality of the inorganic beings in the DMT experience. However, overall he does not know quite enough about *brightness*. He does not realise that unless the actual state of being *in love* is in some sense an aspect of the brightness of an individual it is not really a fully woken brightness – it is not Love-and-Freedom.

* * *

Toward the end of October, 2013, I had a striking dream.

Me and Maysa – my girlfriend – were staying in a rented apartment on holiday in Paris, and it was a sunny winter morning, and there had just been a heavy fall of snow. We looked out of the front door onto a smallish street in the centre of the city, and we looked to the left – the north – and up above us was a very high mountain with a wide ridge covered in trees, and a still quite wide summit, towering above the ridge, that was entirely white with snow. The whole mountain was extremely beautiful, and in the dream I knew that the mountain was a region of Paris – Montmartre.

And the end of the dream was that Maysa said –

"We uncrumple ourselves from our confusion."

21

Two years ago, in Tuva, in hot summer weather, I walked up a high, steep escarpment toward an area of forested mountains. Behind me lower-level expanses of land were stretched out to a far horizon that may have partly consisted of mountains in Mongolia. It was a breathtaking view, that in every way gave the experience of seeing the planet (both the sky and the earth) as opposed to seeing a "country."

It took me three days to get to the forested, sometimes plateau-like mountain-tops – which were spaces of wide summits and high broad valleys, all covered in pine-trees. Arriving there was like getting out onto the "roof" of the country. It felt as if I had found another domain, one more ancient and much less disturbed by human beings, 5000 feet above the first one – a high-level terrain which, looking around me (and remembering the maps I had seen) seemed as if it might cover around a tenth of Tuva.

This other domain was extremely secluded in relation to human beings. All of the paths were animal paths; there was no litter anywhere, and some animals I encountered – two owls, on separate occasions, and a deer – treated me as a curiosity, rather than as a threat (one of the owls flew around me three times, in a circle thirty feet high and a hundred feet across, like an aviator who has discovered something unusual on the ground). The area is secluded in this way because it is exceptionally cold there in winter, and because in summer there is no water other than in small quantities in the very highest places.

I was only able to get to this high-level terrain because two nights before I set out there had been a long overnight thunderstorm with very heavy rain. On the second day of walking I found two rapidly shrinking puddles in a long steep-sided valley which had no stream in it – these puddles were clearly from a recent downpour, that I had experienced just before coming to the mountains. It took me three days and nights to get to the forested "roof-world" of the mountains, and I did it because I vaulted myself up using the water from the puddles. On the first full day of walking – after the initial day of climbing up the escarpment – I got my water from them (using water purification droplets), and then having camped a thousand feet above the place where they were, I went back down the next day to them – now much smaller – and refilled my bottles a second time.

It was after three full days of walking that I reached the point where the ground began to flatten into the forested top of a ridge forming a part of the high-level terrains (at which point I started seeing blueberry bushes everywhere I looked – blueberries were one of the main understory plants of the high forests, and there was a huge quantity of ripe fruit). I camped almost at the top of one of the two main summits in the area that I explored. And it was only the next day that I found out whether or not I would be able to stay for a few days. Three miles beyond the summit, across a broad, relatively shallow forested valley, there was a slightly higher mountain that was much wider and flatter than the first one (it turned out to be an extraordinary labyrinth of forest with occasional glades that sometimes had rock outcrops standing out from them), and my hope was that in the valley between the two summits there would be water. The next day, after the third night in the tent, I walked two miles through the pine-trees – and found a tiny stream, around two feet across.

* * *

Five days before finding the stream, while I was in a small hotel in Tuva's capital, Kyzyl, I had a dream which is worth recounting. Outside there was torrential rain beating down in the streets – a downpour that seemed to last for several hours, and which left the streets partly flooded.

I dreamed that I was in Malton. It was a sunny day (it could have been early morning) and there was no-one around. I was walking toward the bridge over the River Derwent, that leads to the wide space in front of the train station. On my left was a three- storey building (it is a shop called Yates' that sells farming and gardening supplies which has been there for more than a hundred and fifty years, although in the dream there was only an awareness of the building, with no detail). I was walking past the building and approaching the bridge, and as I walked I reached a point where I was seeing the whole of the area in front of the train station. There was no-one there, apart from a single figure two hundred yards away to the extreme left, in an area that had always been a kind of dusty scurf-zone alongside the platform, well away from the station entrance over to the right, an entrance that faces the place where the bridge crosses the river.

The figure was that of a woman – a relatively young woman, wearing a dress, I think, and perhaps the colour of the dress was green, or greyish-green (it was not black, although it was not a bright colour). She was standing facing in my direction, although there was no sense in the dream that she was definitely looking at me. She was too far away for me to see any details of her face, and it was all over in a moment.

In the dream I knew – as if I was being told it as a fact – that the woman was "a rain goddess." There were no details that went with this description, and the jolt of suddenly seeing her in the distance – even though she felt like a positive presence – had a "seeing-a-ghost" effect that immediately woke me up.

I have no inclination to think that what I knew in the dream has a direct connection to the "encounter" involved. In writing about the progressive loss of goddesses from the world of the religions there has been no intention to support the idea of such beings, only the intent to point out the way in which the figure of the female – along with that of the planet – has been pushed back from being a window toward the sacred, toward Love-and-

Freedom.

What can be said is that there was an impersonal quality about the figure's positivity, and a feeling in the dream that in seeing her I was seeing the radically unknown – though she was an unknown with a quality that was more bright and positive than the beings I "encountered" when I was on DMT (for one thing, she was outside, as opposed to occupying a protected, interior space).

The dream also feels like an arrival of a new direction (at that stage the idea of writing about my experiences in Ryedale was two years in the future). It points not just toward Malton, but also toward the planet (pre-eminently it is the planet that brings the rain) and toward women – the two central themes of this writing. There was also an eerie quality about the dream: though she was a positive presence, the figure in the dream was standing at a distance, with no facial contact, so that there was no sense of her being there to reassure me. And if the unknown is there in this sense, then what else might be there?

It is striking to think of the "rain goddess" standing on what would have been the lake-bed of the outflow area of the ancient post-glacial lake. It was here that a gap in the edge of the lake's basin was eroded, so that the lake drained away. And rain and water can only become simultaneously abstract in this context, because it was at the Talbot Hotel that I dreamed about a people in the Andes destroyed by the bursting of their own reservoir ("one night it rained and rained") – a dream which has conducted toward the idea that human beings have been devastated as a result of their own energy-supply having been turned against them.

("curiouser and curiouser," said Alice...)

* * *

It is worth bearing in mind that if dreams to some extent consist of glimpses or views – on the part of an abstract-oneiric perception – then in the face of the radically unknown dreams may be very unfocused. They may for instance attempt to make sense of the unknown by superimposing a known figure (whether it is perceptual or mythological) across the object of the encounter.

* * *

If we uncrumple ourselves we find that the surfaces and organs of the body had been obscuringly folded across the perception, intent, awareness and becomings that are fundamentally what we are. We find also that language (which primarily involves communication) had been folded across the domain of thought, or abstract-perception.

Thought pre-eminently is a world of encounters with the world, and in particular with the real-abstract dimensions of the body without organs (the aspects of the world that consist of intent, freedom, love, lucidity, reason, improvisation, structure, feeling, becomings etc.). Thought overall engages both with singularities (encountered individual beings) perceived primarily as non-concrete or as abstract worlds of the body without organs, and it engages with the multi-instance lines or currents that transect the spatium of beings.

Three further intent-currents have now come into the foreground. They are perception, the entirety of the self, and awareness.

The entirety of the self is another name for the entirety of the body. The self – or body – in its entirety is the body without organs together with the body *with* organs (which in fact is a world of energy and in the last analysis is not different from the first aspect, just more locked-down). And it is vital to see that the body without organs is intent, and that it is a world of becomings. Intent is Love-and-Freedom, and love – is a dance of becomings, maintained in existence by freedom, by avoidance of domination by will-to-control (to travel toward the infinity of Love-and-Freedom beyond us is not domination by will-to-control).

Awareness is an ability to take in memories. These virtual-real worlds provide guidance (they are like eyes or lenses through which we can see the world), but they are also – while the control-mind is in effect – like a submerged world beneath us that drains our energy and limits our action. Our awareness-world is not at all who we are: we are a singular world of intent, perception, love, lucidity, becomings, fascination, hostility to attack – and none of these has anything to do with the contingent world of what has happened to us. Memory-worlds are a summit of the mountain of history, and although at the right time it can be very valuable to see from one its vantages, it is necessary to not become trapped by the baleful, attractive power of this mountain.

Perception is both that of the body with organs, and of the body *without* organs. And in relation to the second aspect there is both abstract perception and abstract-oneiric perception (as has been seen both dreamings – story-worlds – and dreams in sleep are also eyes or lenses through which we see the world). But notwithstanding the immense importance of these other forms of perception, it may well be that initially our main efforts need to be directed at waking perception in the usual sense of the term. This is because almost the whole of the physical body – as opposed to the intent body – has been ignored and betrayed in favour of a tiny fraction of what lies beyond it, and in favour of a fraction of what it includes (together these elements are a cluster made up of blocked-reason, sex, language, and control-behaviour). As a result of this situation we are awash with words, and with a slew of indulgent, dysfunctional and unnec-essary habitual actions. To concentrate on perception – and on other physical-body aspects, such as breathing, and patterns of actions – is therefore a waking of the body *with* organs that is both a waking of perception (which is not in the end separable at all from abstract perception, as when you see the intent of someone when they are in front of you) and a freeing up of energy that will now be available for the waking of the entirety of the body, the entirety of the self.

* * *

This writing is immensely indebted to the work of Gilles Deleuze. However, it should be said immediately that the problem with Deleuze is that in – momentously – breaking open a view toward the body without organs within his conceptual field he does not point out how eerie it is to look in this direction: there is generally no suggestion of how it seems human beings are being stalked in ways that fundamentally involve this depth-dimension of the world.

There is a contrasting – although not at all symmetrical – problem with the work of William Burroughs, which is vitiated by being almost entirely gothic, which is to say that having arrived in the spatium of the body without organs, Burroughs's focus is primarily locked in the direction of the gothic aspect of the unknown. In the language of *A Thousand Plateaus*, Burroughs is an instance of a "captured nomad war machine" – but captured by a disguised gravity of the control-mind, as opposed to the state, in the sense that he has turned to fight and cannot turn away and gain a sustained view of the "bright-transcendental"(and start travelling implacably toward it, which is also the only way of fighting). Burroughs is an example of a writer with an intense sense of humour who produces an illusion of seeing through everything, while writing from a blocked perspective: the danger of comedy is an oneiric mode which is stultified by gravity and confusion (the bleak atmosphere created by a writer like Tom Sharpe is a non-visionary, oneiric cynicism in comparison – a very distant relative).

However, returning to the main issue, the eerie is faintly present within the work of Deleuze, as with the descriptions in *Difference and Repetition* of the metamorphoses of Oedipus in *Oedipus at Colonus* (the play ignored by blocked modernism, as opposed to *Oedipus Rex*) and of Hamlet[39] – Hamlet who says "there are more things in heaven and earth [...] than are dreamt of in your philosophy." And the combination of Deleuze and Felix Guattari in *A Thousand Plateaus* takes everything much further, as with the descriptions of the becomings-animal of sorcery knowledge-worlds in the tenth section of this book, and the moment where the entirety of the self is evoked, with the help of a paraphrase-section drawing upon Pierrette Fleutiaux's *The Story of the Telescope and the Abyss*:

"One day [...you will...] start walking across a narrow overpass above the dark abyss [...] on a line of flight to meet a blind Double approaching from the other side."[40]

But in the end the potential for the eerie is insistent and ambient simply because a seeing of the body without organs entails a seeing of the world around you as not different in kind from yourself – and therefore as an eerie world of the unknown that consists of intent, feeling and awareness (a transcendental "out there" in which unknown elements could be interested in our energy, or could be interested in entering into becoming with us/drawing us forward). And despite the somewhat distracting tone created by language drawn from science and social science the book is not at all fixated upon life-forms in relation to the dimensions of energy and awareness. Section 10 – in which they start a sentence with the phrase "we sorcerers"[41] – states that becoming-woman is the starting point for the process of waking becomings, but the final clause of the section title "... becoming-imperceptible" is about entering into envisaging-composition with non-lifeform elements ("it is necessary to choose the right molecule" [42]): the section is a handbook for entering into "disembodied intercourse with the sky," to quote Virginia Woolf[43], a guide to entering into becoming with the wider, transcendental worlds of intent and awareness of the planet, and of what is beyond the planet.

A Thousand Plateaus is therefore a spectacular philosophical breakthrough at the end of the high-intensity phase from 1962 to 1982 (an era during which the power of blocked modernism made it hard for dreamings, as opposed to songs, despite all the available energy, and despite the occasional exceptions, like *Picnic at Hanging Rock*). Along with Spinoza's *Ethics* and *Thus Spoke Zarathustra* it is one of the most lucid and powerful of the works of western philosophy, though it is maybe a good thing to remember that its subtitle, "Capitalism and Schizophrenia," is misleading in relation to the book's systems of outsights, which despite all the critique, is pre-eminently directed toward the worlds and dimensions beyond ordinary, denuded reality - "In short, we think that one cannot write sufficiently in the name of an outside"[44] (and it is also worth remembering that another momentous book of capitalism and schizophrenia is Barbara O'Brien's *Operators and Things*). And a final point is that the book's demolition of Freudianism in its opening chapter is a part of a precise, effective analysis that induces toward freedom in coming to understand and wake the faculties of dreaming and perception.

* * *

The vantage of this writing on the "mountain" of history has been the end of the phase from 1962 to 1982. And of course in relation to the planet the vantage on the one hand has been Ryedale/the North York Moors, and on the other, the vague, indeterminate sprawl of zones that is named by the phrase "the western world".

It is worth seeing that although Britain has been a main focus, so have France, Mexico and America, and to a lesser extent, Germany and Australia (but even this is to simplify, given that Tuva has also been involved, along with Patagonia and New Zealand).

Regarding the time-perspective, the fundamental issue is to see this as about an attunement for the purposes of travelling toward the Outside – the Future – rather than as a story about the heroic rise-and-then-collapse of a human domain, which "nearly made it", but failed again. Overall the situation is not that different during times of high-intensity: and it is not just that these times are most accurately seen as traps for the unwary (who become dynamically trapped in dead-gestures of flailing against the religio-social establishment – the ecumenon) but that they are also times when many people simply use the available energy for the decorating of forms of slow-collapse capitulation. The vital thing is to point out that the Future has been alongside all along, and a way of doing this is to see toward the Future by looking through the doorway of a particular time.

* * *

I did not notice the collapse when it happened. It was too gradual, and I was too embroiled in my own collapse into recurrent wage-slavery and self-doubt. I very definitely *felt* it, but I did not bring it to the point of it being an element of thought (and then I found a line of flight which in a better way prevented me from noticing the event).

Later I started to be strongly aware of an earlier decline, although one that was not really at all a falling-away in the same sense, although it was a precursor, a major shift. At some point in the mid-eighties I started to say to people that in thinking about the time I first started listening to pop-rock music, around 1973, I had the vague impression that at that time I had just missed a gigantic party (this statement was sometimes met with complete antipathy).

I had this overall – intensifying – impression of a party-that-ended to a great extent because of the Beatles. It is telling that despite the Beatles being three years in the past in 1973 it was their music that made the greatest impact on me (the first album I bought was the 67-70 double album, and I went back the next day and bought the 62-67 album). The emphasis and descriptions of the first book of cultural history I read – Philip Norman's book about the Beatles, *Shout*, which I read in 1983 – would only heighten this impression.

However, a little later again, the overall picture would come into focus. The transition all along had been a shift from a large-scale "solar-trance" exuberance (the predominant mode of the 60s) to a "cosmic-trance" exuberance which as such was both "solar-trance" and "night-trance" ("In the night, in the eye of the forest" – Patti Smith, 1975) and which, while being fundamentally expansive for those swept up into it, affected far fewer people in a direct way. After 1970 it is primarily only the wild kids who remain – though wildness here covers a spectrum of courage and has nothing to do with being aggressively icono-clastic (you should not think just about punk or post-punk – you should also have in mind Stevie Nicks and her song Rhiannon, and Kate Bush).

It was a while before the real collapse began to be noticed. I felt something "retrograde" about The Police (which had nothing to do with their reggae aspect), and I felt the strangeness, around 1983, of pop suddenly seeming to have been invaded by Elvis impersonators and people with a singing style from the 1950s (Shakin Stevens; and the Paul Young of Uptown Girl, which evidently is a fine track, but...). And maybe most of all I felt a kind of ambient multi-tone melancholy both in music that had high kudos (I Don't Like Mondays, Going Underground) and in low-kudos tracks like Video Killed the Radio Stars, and ELO's

1982 album Time, a concept- album about a man trapped and unhappy in the future, a future from which he is unable to escape.

At the adult education college to which I went in north Wales – Coleg Harlech – I managed to live for two years in a protective bubble of relatively unblocked modernism: it was a place that dreamers of heightened futures – like HG Wells or the Marge Piercy of the novel *Woman on the Edge of Time* – would have liked very much, whatever its problems. Its modernism was there in its motto coming from the *Mabinogion* – "Avo Penn Bid Pont" (if you would be a leader be a bridge) - and in a pervasive Marxist socialism that was extremely open to all forms of literature that did not adhere to the mythos-worlds of territory and religion. And for me Coleg Harlech and Shakespeare both "arrived" at the same time – when I went for the interview I also went to see a performance in the college theatre by a touring company of Twelfth Night (a performance which made a big impression on me, and was the first Shakespeare play I had seen). There were extraordinary people around (amongst many others these included Neil Jinks from Scritti Politti, living in Harlech because his girlfriend was at the college); there were mountains and a five mile sandy beach with a huge area of dunes; but it was not clear to me at the time that I was living in a protection-zone with other refugees from 62-82. When I left I saw a bleak piece of graffiti in a room whose posters had been taken down, and remembered that I had seen it two years before when I came for my interview. It said "Do not adjust your minds, reality is out of focus."

It was only afterwards that the real shock came. It was the autumn term at Oxford, in 1986 (I left Oxford after two terms, and then went on, after a two-year gap, to get my degree at Warwick), and I was listening to The Smiths with two friends who would both have been around 18. The Smiths were being presented to me by both of them as the outer-edge of musical brilliance, and although I liked the guitar playing very much and recognised the overall talent, I felt strongly that there was something wrong (though I didn't say anything). I was sensing a melancholy pose, passing itself off as profundity: a very impressively talented musical affectation, both in the words and in the tone of the singing.

The lines of flight still exist during phases of low intensity: for a while there was Kate Bush, and soon there was drum and bass, and bands like The Cure and Radiohead (though these songs tended to be personal in their emphasis, with a bleakness that usually only had a transcendental edge through the feeling in the songs of the background radiation of sadness). And along with rare astonishing breakthroughs – like *The Pick, The Sickle and the Shovel*, by Gravediggaz, and the songs of both Rosario Blefari and Juana Molina in Argentina – there was the ongoing pulse of dub-reggae, that had been there from long before the collapse, and that has gone on all the way to become dubstep. It is interesting that when in 1984 William Gibson achieves a real abstract-oneiric escape with *Neuromancer* (an achievement from which he has steadily fallen away in successive novels) the book is threaded with references to this zone of music. One of the last chapters of the book ends with Case – the main character – crossing over into sleep while listening to "the long pulse of Zion dub"

* * *

It is the beginning of 1978. Althea and Donna's Uptown Top-Ranking is number one ("Pop ain't got no style, I's strictly roots"). Punk had shattered pop-rock, and now the remaining "mainstream" bands in England were largely talentless (like The Brotherhood of Man), and punk itself was not strong enough – or inspired enough – to take over. While new directions started to emerge beneath the surface the only development that kept the impression that it was all alright was the emergence of Kate Bush, together with the songs like Northern Lights and Automatic Lover that had very little impact on the charts. In 1978 there are almost no songs by British bands that reach number one – apart from Wuthering Heights there is only "Matchstick Men" and 10CCs I-don't-like-cricket song "Dreadlock Holiday" (this song is a deterioration from the oneiric courage of "I'm Mandy, Fly Me", from 1976).

(But it was not all over – post-punk in all its forms was about to happen: from Siouxsie and the Banshees to Scritti Politti, from The Jam to Ari Upp singing with The New Age Steppers).

* * *

In the world of abstract-oneiric works what happens around 1978 is extraordinary. As has been seen, strange tales are intrinsically expressions of (glimpses and sustained views of) the second sphere of action. And now, after it has been suppressed through the earlier course of the phase of high intensity, the strange tale bursts into life, either in straightforward forms, or ones which are liminal or "fractured". Along with Donaldson's three books, there is Robert Holdstock's *Mythago Wood* (1979), Le Guin's *The Beginning Place* (1979), John Foxx's *The Quiet Man* (1980), and Hammond's *Sapphire and Steel* (1979-81). At the same time Doris Lessing leaves behind "realist" fiction and starts – in 1978 – to write a series of five "fractured" strange-tale novels, which contain many dislocated elements of the strange tale while being overcoded by a known dimension of wise aliens (meaning that in place of the wall of the unknown there are the known super-developed aliens, who to a great extent are a kind of delerial, though empirical equivalent to the dogmatic-delirium elements of religions).

It is also important to point out that *The Shining* (1977) also has aspects of the strange tale. The other – crowded – ballroom in which Jack Torrence talks to the bartender in the hotel is not less real than the empty ballroom that someone with no faculty of "shining" might see at this point, with Jack standing talking in an empty room. It is this that Gibson remembers in *Neuromancer* when Case arrives on the empty beach with the derelict buildings in the distance (sea to the left, and an unknown space of dunes to the right) and for a while he has the sinister figure of the bartender Ratz walking with him, undermining him by suggesting he has all along been trying to kill himself.[45]

* * *

At the "centre" of all this, beyond all the popularity-charts and kudos-systems of 1978 I see two views. I see a preternaturally beautiful and immense expanse of solar-trance and night-trance terrains, suffused in sunlight – with only a few people occupying a world of wilderness countryside that is faced calmly outward toward an unknown located to the South. And I see the people who are focused on the flows of the social-field becoming aware of how icy calm they will have to be (reticent and immovable in meeting provocations) if they are to keep their love awake, and keep travelling outward toward this South horizon.

* * *

Of all of the *sequences* of stays in hotels in the year from October 1977 to October 1978 I remember almost nothing. Despite (or because of) the intensity of the events that took place, the stays at the Talbot Hotel in the spring of 1978 are completely unconnected from memories of other hotels, apart from the knowledge that with the first of them when I arrived it was not long since I had been in Swansea, at a seven-storey hotel in the centre of the city, called the Dragon. I do not even remember how many of these visits to the Talbot there were at this time (two, three?). There is a very similar lack of "sequence" memories with the later visits to the Black Swan (I do remember that at one point we went on to the Golden Fleece at Thirsk). But with the first visit to the Black Swan there is a very long sequence.

It seems that this memory is about a letting go toward acceptance of my new bizarre situation (hotel nomadism), and, at a deeper level, a letting go both toward the planet, and toward my enigmatic line of flight, at this time – my love of winter. It was as if the Black Swan Hotel and the snow that fell on it and around it together became a "friend" that gave me enough security and joy to ensure that in a prolonged way I gave up worrying and let myself perceive and dream (and such a letting go always gives an energy that leads to effective action – during that stay I stopped being upset about not writing to my sister, and instead sent her a long letter and a present).

* * *

At the beginning of the sequence I was staying, in mid-December, at a pleasant but not impressive hotel in Corbridge in Northumberland (I remember standing at dusk on the bridge over the Tyne, looking upstream, and feeling that I had been staying in hotels for a long time). We then went to the Beaumont Hotel, ten miles to the west, in Hexham, and I remember really liking this hotel, and feeling a warmth about it, with its tall labyrinth of rooms (it was part of a terrace of four or five storey buildings), multiple staircases and its westward views over a park near the centre of the town. After this we travelled down an exceptionally beautiful secluded valley in the southwest of Northumberland (I think it is perhaps a valley that I have seen on the map that runs north-south "alongside" the valley of the South Tyne), and stayed for a few days in a hotel in Borrodale in the Lake District (my mother was visiting a friend who lived at a farm in Buttermere, by the lake which has given the village its name). After that we stayed at a hotel in Bradford (where I remember taking in the lightness and intelligent warmth of a Doonesbury cartoon for the first time, and feeling that I had been seeing these cartoons for a while, though without really focusing on them). Then we went on to a hotel called the Clarendon in Leamington Spa, in Warwickshire. I really liked Leamington, but I couldn't quite work out why. I thought maybe its grid of streets reminded me of Christchurch, but I knew there was something more than good associations.

After that we headed for the Fosse Way, three miles to the east of the town– the Roman road – and travelled southwest to Newton Abbot in Devon (my mother had one distant relative, and a friend, who both lived a few miles away from the town), staying for about five days in a hotel in the centre of the town. We spent Christmas there, in an atmosphere that somehow I found a little bleak and oppressive. There was a feeling of things being in some sense *wrong* – a feeling that was interrupted but not dispelled by a trip to Widdicombe when I climbed up a hill in frosty weather and saw snow on the tops of the moors (on this walk I remember I was thinking at one point about the prolonged firemans' strike that was taking place, although I don't remember what I was thinking). Towards the end of the stay I had a row with my mother and ended up walking west out of the town toward the countryside, thinking seriously – in some sense of the word – that I was going to keep walking and find some way of escaping the bizarre hotel-saga in which I found myself, with no end in sight.

During the evenings and nights at the hotel I saw a series of three sci-fi films, which I loved, but which at the same time gave me a feeling of dissatisfaction. They were the comic precursor to *Alien*, Carpenter and O'Bannon's 1974 film *Dark Star*, the impressive but melancholic *Silent Running*, and a low-budget sci-fi musical about a group of alternative-culture people, led by a man called Hoan, who escape a total destruction of the Earth in a spaceship and set off toward a star in the constellation Orion. A "bad" member of the crew – a man – is overcome and killed in a fight with Hoan, and the musical featured a song in the middle and at the end with the chorus "Guide us, Orion!"

I was very prepared to be in love with science fiction, but somehow it never had this effect, even though in different ways I enjoyed all three of these films. I had enjoyed them, but simultaneously I was left with a cloying taste of melancholy and affectation (this situation was not improved later that year when I went to see Star Wars at the cinema: the aftertaste of "Americanist" heroism-affectation was very strong, especially after the final medal-giving scene, and when everyone stood up to clap at the end I remained sitting down).

From Newton Abbot we travelled all the way – around four hundred miles – to the Worsley Arms, in Hovingham, where we stayed for two or three nights, and where one day there was a light fall of snow through which I walked up the road by which I camped when I returned to the area, in the summer of 2013. And then after that we went six miles up the road to the Black Swan, for the start of the new year, and I felt from the first morning, when it snowed, that I had arrived somewhere that was the *right* place: it was the heartening, secure place – warm, and deep inside the winter – that somehow I needed, to sort myself out.

What was this line of flight of my love of winter? It was at this stage very much a planetary love – a love of the planet in one of its startlingly beautiful modes – but it had initially been inculcated into me by oneiric forces that were partly planetary but were also melancholic and religious. A love of "north" and of winter, and of the Christian blocked dreaming is a very dangerous thing: a subtle, serenely capitulatory affect - "we who understand must not have the arrogance to be expansive but must calmly and kindly huddle together in our homes that face the cosmic sadness of the physical world – for who could have the arrogance to think they could fight the blizzard of this vale of tears?" Unfocused "poetic-mythic" sorrow and defeatism has many apparently lovely manifestations, but this is one of the most seductive and dangerous. In the three or four years after 1979 the tone of my love of winter would become more melancholic, but then, around the time of Coleg Harlech, and the "arrival" of Shakespeare, I began to be turned toward summer and the south, with my still-existing love of winter now taking up a place in the background instead of in the centre.

But for that time, at the Black Swan, it was pure planetary line of flight, with nothing deleterious about it. It was perceptual joy. And the whole hotel and town and secluded valley was perceptual joy in the same way (it can be seen why five years later at Coleg Harlech, looking back, I did the automatic writing that was the poem Haven in Winter, a poem which was primarily about that stay at the Black Swan).

* * *

During this stay, I would have seen the first episode of *Blake's Seven* (I remember seeing it, and it was broadcast on 2nd of January) and I am fairly sure that I saw the second episode at the hotel as well, in its ancient TV room by the churchyard. I didn't really try very hard to watch the series after this (I think I saw a few more episodes of the first series, and then there were very long gaps, so probably I only saw a tenth of the total run).

Although I recognised its weaknesses and poor production values, the series did not leave me with a bad aftertaste. I was not in any sense in love with it (the way I was in love for a while with Bladerunner, the first sci-fi film to profoundly affect me, with its very contrasted reference to Orion, and its haunting awareness that we are all going to die), but somehow, with all its appalling messiness, *Blake's Seven* was a valuable dreaming. At some level of awareness I liked its anti-establishment "internationalism": it involved a group of rebels from different worlds, rather than a group of state representatives, as with Star Trek, and I liked the strangeness and believability of it having a – partially – sympathetic but grimly ruthless machiavel as a central figure in the group of rebels. And although I remember no direct connections to what I started doing, the sci-fi optic it helped to create went smoothly into my enjoyment of the Black Swan: it was not that this optic was an "anachronistic" anomaly kept separate in the TV room – on the contrary, parts of the hotel started to be transformed in my mind into rooms on a spaceship (I remember this happening with the room I had during that visit, a room which I am fairly sure I did not have again). The spaces of these envisaged worlds had a lonely-yet-secure quality – rather than the affect of a rebel-group space drama – but *Blake's Seven* was likely to have been involved in this development at the level of the "virtual real" within the hotel.

It feels as if after the Black Swan I became a bit more calm and pragmatic – the planetary line of flight (my love for the planet in the form of my love of winter) had woken a little, and to a small extent I was stronger, more capable of the departures that were possible in the circumstances.

I don't remember much of January and February, apart from the fact that at one point I travelled by train from Northumberland to London in order to go to a Pickfords warehouse in Westham, to arrange for the furniture and belongings from the house in New Zealand to be sent to a warehouse in York (my mother had given me a cheque). Because my mother had not asked me to send everything from New Zealand she said I should do all the work, including – subsequently – sending monthly cheques to York, to pay for the boxes and furniture being kept in long-term storage.

Around the middle of March I was in Swansea, and I bought a small portable radio (it seems likely I bought it because I had seen Kate Bush singing Wuthering Heights on TV). The radio put me back in touch with the pop-rock world, and at exactly the same time, in Swansea, I read a Stephen King introduction to one of his books (at that time there were only three) where I was struck by the intelligence of his writing. The abstract-oneiric in the form of modern horror was now about to arrive as well (it was probably only a week later that I read *The Shining* at the Talbot).

I intensely enjoyed both the spring and the summer (as if I was already beginning the turn toward Summer, away from the fixation on Winter). The summer of 1978 was not particularly good, but there were several long spells of hot sunny weather, and it was not a summer of recurrent rain.

The second thing I added, after buying a radio (bought with some of the last of the money I had saved when I had been working full-time in a shop in New Zealand) was my bicycle, which I retrieved from the warehouse in York. It feels as if it was May, or early June.

I started cycling from hotel to hotel, one of the few innovations of which I was capable, cycling up to seventy miles in a day. That summer we stayed mostly in Yorkshire and Northumberland so the innovation worked very well, for a while. I was often cycling through beautiful countryside, and I had found a minimal degree of independence.

* * *

But at a point later in the summer the new poise I had reached received a jolt, whose effects did not completely go away. During a stay at the Anchor Hotel I had a heated argument with my mother about her refusal to sign the power of attorney that would allow my sister to sell the house in New Zealand (there was a small zoo near the hotel, and I remember going to ask the man who ran the zoo if he needed someone to work there). My mother's refusal was old news, it had not been open for discussion since the very beginning, when I had arrived from

New Zealand. But the upshot of the argument was that I refused to keep sending the cheques to the warehouse.

My "going on strike" in this way did not cause her to send the cheques (and I think I always felt this would be the case): instead no more cheques were ever sent, and the belongings from New Zealand were simply abandoned. I think maybe the warehouse had no means of contacting us, but in any case, we never saw any of those possessions again (presumably after a few months they were sold). I didn't give a large amount of thought to it (although I was distressed when I did think about it), and the fact that I didn't is maybe a sign that a part of me was content to let go of it all. What is evident however, is that in jettisoning this household of objects a force had been removed that had been impelling us towards finding a house (and staying there once it had been found). We were now "travelling light" and through three winter lets, and one two-year stay in a house, we kept being able to load most things into the car, and keep moving (there was occasional use of sheds and outhouses belonging to friends of my mother).

But despite this outcome in some sense being a positive one, I was aware that what had triggered it had been a kind of angry petulance on my part. As autumn started I had a sexual self-doubt, combined with a self-doubt involving what had happened with our belongings, and a renewed distress concerning my infrequent letters to my sister.

I remember cycling to Northumberland to a hotel by the motorway, called, I think, the Tyneside Posthouse.It was not an attractive place: the upland of semi-industrial terrain around it was windswept and without an inspiring atmosphere, even though I loved motorways. I remember being a bit unhappy and stressed while I was there. I know that the cycling was about to come to an end – at some point after this we started doing journeys that were too long, and the bicycle had to be put in the car. Not long afterwards it was stored in the garage of a friend of my mother who lived to the south of Skipton.

It was the beginning of autumn. The autumn of the broadcast of the TV version of *No-Mans Land*, and of the first performance of *Betrayal* (a play where Pinter simply uses realism – though with a reversed chronological sequence – to show something very bleak about a recurrent form of romantic relationship). It was the autumn of Justin Hayward's song Forever Autumn, with its connection to a dreaming of planetary desolation as a result of an invasion of aliens (the song comes from the 1978 album *Jeff Wayne's The War of the Worlds*), and of *Systems of Romance*, about which it should be said – having invoked the music already – that the title and album cover are together an amazing moment of deep-level critique. The women had kept it all alive through the summer, but in the overall social field (which abuts tightly upon the ecumenon) there was now a change in tone, an addition of a feeling of something oppressive, a feeling of a fight or "survival-struggle" beginning to take place.

I had a powerful dream while I was at the hotel, but I could remember only a few details. The dream was a bit like watching a film, although it had the odd property of there being rhythmic "voice-over" words that went with it, so that the film was also like a song. I was dreaming that I was seeing a group of people escaping from a gigantic and labyrinthine city that seemed both absolutely present-day, but also medieval, or from the time of Shakespeare. Everything was in bright sunlight (though I feel it was evening sunlight) and there was a lightness and humour and depth-of-knowledge – and beauty – about it all that afterwards I tantalisingly remembered without being able to hold on to the details. In the dream the people escaped, and the last part of the rhythmic speech-accompaniment was the statement that they escaped "through apple-door – and gate-guard". The word apple-door was simultaneously the word Appledore (I have only just found out that this is the name of a village on the west side of North Devon, opposite the town Westward Ho), and the idea with "gate-guard" seemed to be that they had got away through the help of the gate-guard (whoever or whatever that was). The final image was a view from somewhere in countryside on the west coast of the island (maybe Wales) where I saw the group of people disappearing into the sky to the west, looking like birds rather than humans. They were in the far distance, and disappeared almost immediately, and the image, although it was of humans being seen as birds, seemed schematic or abstract – there was no quality of amazement at seeing humans who could fly (the image was simultaneously as revealing and evidently cryptic as the words, although affectively it had a simple, intense beauty and sadness – they had made it, I had been left behind).

As with the earlier dream, at the Talbot, about the people in the Andes, I did a drawing with the words underneath, to retain as much of the dream as I could. In both cases I was very dissatisfied with the result, but the drawings nonetheless probably achieved part of their purpose.

At that time I did not remember many dreams, but when I did remember them there was a slight tendency for them to involve beautiful, bright, planetary places (as opposed to interiors), and for them to not involve me speaking to people. When I went to Coleg Harlech and at last had a peer-group to whom I had to "explain myself" I was struck by the way in which I was suddenly talking all the time in my dreams.

The last event to be included in this context is a dream that took place around 1981, in the house where we stayed for two years, about four miles east of Malton. I dreamed that I was watching, and also somehow taking part in, events in a space-station (the atmosphere was a little like *Alien*, a film I had not seen) where the crew in some way were fated – perhaps unless they re-routed themselves onto a different parallel time – in several years from the present to become hideous malevolent husks of themselves, space-station zombies. And in the dream a voice-over (which in fact was like the voice-over of a trailer) was explaining that the future selves would find a way of getting into the present with the aim of killing their original forms. And at the end of the dream I was standing in a long, badly-lit space-station passageway (the space-station was now badly damaged) with my three friends and fellow crew-members, and in the distance at the end of the passageway a line of four shambling figures was appearing, just far enough away for me to be not quite able to see for sure that one of them was my future self. And as I woke up the voice-over was saying its slogan for the film – "When the future comes hunting for the past."

* * *

My memories of the Talbot Hotel are somehow of a different kind in relation to those about the Black Swan. They are brighter, more open to the south horizon (this relates in part to an actual topographic difference between Malton and Helmsley), and are more about summer, and being in love. It seems important to point out here that, fifteen years later, when I dreamed about the hauntingly beautiful group of people (friends, escape-comrades, explorers of reality) living in a house in some woodland, in the first dream the house was near Hovingham (which is halfway to Helmsley), whereas it was in the more detailed and powerful dreams (which also maintained consistency with each other) that it was in the woodland to the southwest of Malton.

My dreaming created a forest in a part of the south horizon, viewed from the Talbot, and it created a house in the middle of this woodland, by a small lake. It is a hidden place in a beautiful area, away from a zone of seclusion around Helmsley that was perhaps a little too affected by the presence of elements in the terrain that are connected to a major fault-line in the blocked dreamings of the English ecumenon: these elements, as has been pointed out, being Castle Howard (with its demolished Temple of Venus, and its re-named Temple of Diana), the catholic public school, Ampleforth College, together with Ampleforth Abbey, and the ruined abbeys of Rievaulx and Byland.

During my return-visit to Ryedale, after the night near Hovingham – I was not thinking about the dreams, when I camped in that area – I went to Helmsley on footpaths that led across a footbridge over the Rye, and I was in Helmsley on two successive days, camping for a night on a wooded hill five miles to the west. After it being sunny on arrival in Helmsley there was then heavy rain, which was only really coming to an end as I set out toward Bransdale on the second day. On the third day – which was a day of warm sunshine – I walked through the top of Bransdale, across Farndale, stopping for coffee there in a village pub, and then I walked into Rosedale and down the entire length of the dale. It had been a hot summer, and as well as finding large quantities of wild raspberries, strawberries and blueberries, I also found two bushes covered in green-gold gooseberries, that were so sun-ripened they were delicious eaten raw.

On the last morning I had camped in a narrow stretch of woodland at the top of a hill facing out over Ryedale. It was sunny with very clear air, and I was walking across a large stubble field, with big cylinders of straw-bales, slightly nervous because I knew I had been camping without permission and was trespassing. And then I looked up at the view. In the distance, beyond and around Malton, were the slopes of the wolds, with a lucid world of bright summer sky above them. To the southwest there was a very tall cloud of smoke, from somewhere over the horizon, which was white in the sunlight, and which I guessed was probably the smoke from a large quantity of burning unwanted straw, rising slowly upwards in the windless conditions, perhaps drawn by thermals, creating a plume as high as a storm-cloud. In front of me there was a wide wraith of white-grey mist, not far from ground level, covering most of the part of the Vale of Pickering that was potentially in sight, a wraith of mist that was extremely suggestive of the lake that once covered the area. In the middle distance, rising bizarrely out of this mist-cloud, were the rollercoaster of a fun park called Flamingo Land, together with some other tall fairground ride (initially I thought I was seeing farm silos of some unusual kind, and then I realised that it was the fun park). To my right there was a bright diagonal section of a road, with cars on it, which went to the top of a low hill in the near distance, then out of sight – it was the road to Kirkbymoorside, the market town between Pickering (which was visible four miles away to the left) and Helmsley, another eight miles to the west.

The sky was astonishing in the clear light, and so was the expanse of low mist, lit up by the sun.

It was the planetary view. The view where suddenly you are seeing a terrain of sky and land, and you are seeing it not as a part of a country, but as a captivatingly beautiful space of the planet. It was like the view in Tuva, the view toward Mongolia from the top of the initial 3000 foot escarpment of the mountains.

On one side, the system of reason-revelation involves the domains of maths and science, and on the other it firstly involves "sacred territories" - whose sacredness comes from being gifts from an extrinsic, non-earthly divine being or force, or from being associated with such a force – and, secondly, the leaders and heroes of these terrains who are associated with the extrinsic divine force (leaders, monarchs, scientists, poets, priests, "war-heroes" etc). It is a system of "grandeur" that has captured a little of the glow of the bright-transcendental – Love-and-Freedom – but which gives the impression the glow comes from a different place in relation to its actual source. From the idea of scientific laws obeyed by nature, to the ideas of God, and of Platonic truths there is always a fending off of the planet (and of the female).

In this way the system of reason-revelation allows people to draw their energy (pre-eminently from the planet and from women) through mediating channels involving a contempt for the earthly and the "frivolously-female" in favour of a delusion-world of religious dreamings, and in favour of a fixation on a tiny bandwidth of abstraction in the form of the frozen and repetitive "regular" zones (with their eternal truths) that are the area of engagement of a constricted form of reason.

It is necessary to reach the lucidity beyond reason-revelation, and it is necessary to stop despising what we love, to stop despising the worlds from which all along we draw our energy:

"Only if one loves this earth with unbending passion can one release one's sadness [...]. The sadness belongs only to those who hate the very thing that gives shelter to their beings.[46]

All of this therefore is to say that the oneiric entrapment-worlds of territorial and religious allegiances have to be left behind in the direction of the planet, and in the direction of becomings – and first and foremost, becoming-woman.

The lightness and twirling, playful brightness of women is momentous sensual intensity but without sex being involved: it is an intense distributed joy entirely without affectation or ulterior governance – a quiet female bliss of free, creative movement. Brightness is the way forward, a male brightness as well as a female brightness – a question of being beyond grave judgements, outrage, kudos-fixation, and the self-importance of taking offence at people's actions. Here there also needs to be a sustained, scrutinising concentration on the intent of what you are encountering, both in relation to the senses, and in the wider (external and internal) world of the abstract-oneiric systems. And this improvisatory, disciplined spontaneity (a state of woken perception, free of unnecessary internal verbalising) is inseparably a heightened encounter with the planet.

* * *

To travel into the unknown is a sober-joyful process of gaining energy by overcoming self-importance, and by eradicating all forms of self-indulgence – and it is a development of the ability to have effective, creative comradeship-alliances with other human beings. It is a process of perceiving – and dreaming – a way toward wider spaces of existence.

Beyond the ongoing disaster of ordinary reality is the second sphere of action. You don't get to be there on a sustained basis unless in some sense you are part of a group, and a group can only form (no plan is possible, only continuous improvisation) if you have learned to let yourself be swept away into the intent-currents of Love-and-Freedom that run through the world – intent-currents that take you South, into the Future.

Notes

1. Deleuze and Guattari make extensive use of the concept of the body without organs in *A Thousand Plateaus* and *Anti-Oedipus*. The concept relates in different senses to the whole of the world, but for the purposes of orientation it can be pointed out that the body without organs of a human individual – or a human group – consists of intent, love, lucidity, awareness, envisaging, anticipation, energy, dreams, feeling, reason etc.

2. p. 42. Barbara O'Brien, *Operators and Things*, London: Sphere Books Ltd, 1976.

3. Act 2, Scene 1, from line 123.

4. p. 55, Friedrich Nietzsche, *Thus Spoke Zarathustra*, Part 1, *Of the Three Metamorphoses*, London: Penguin, 1969.

5. Peter Shaffer, *Equus*, p.62 and p.83, London: London, 2006.

6. pp. 99-107, Gilles Deleuze, *Essays Critical and Clinical*, Verso, London, 1998.

7. From en.wikipedia.org/wiki/The_Eye_of_the_Heron, cited as from "Coming back from the silence (interview with Ursula Le Guin)," *Whole Earth Review*, Spring, 1995.

8. p. 73, Gilles Deleuze and Felix Guattari, *A Thousand Plateaus*, London: Athlone, 1988.

9. As cited above, p.22.

10. 23-30, Carlos Castaneda, *The Fire from Within*, New York: Simon and Schuster,1984.

11. pp. 83-84, Spinoza, *Ethics*, London: J.M.Dent, 1993.

12. p. 469, Stephen Donaldson, *The Chronicles of Thomas Covenant, the Unbeliever*, London: Harper Collins, 1996.

13. pp. 48-49, Harold Pinter, *No Man's Land*, London: Faber and Faber, 1991.

14. As cited above, pp.85-86.

15. p.362, Francois Dosse, *Intersecting Lives*, New York:

Columbia University Press, 2010.

16. p. xx (preface), Gilles Deleuze, *Difference and Repetition*, London: Athlone, 1994.

17. Bob Dylan, Gates of Eden, from *Bringing it all Back Home*, released March 27th, 1965.

18. p. 90, Richard Adams, *Watership Down*, London: Penguin, 1973.

19. Section 28, p. 31, Lao Tzu, *Tao Te Ching*, translated by David Hinton, Berkeley, Counterpoint, 2002.

20. As cited above, section 10, p. 12.

21. As cited above, section 6, p. 8.

22. p.247, Florinda Donner, *Being-in-Dreaming*, New York: Harper Collins, 1991.

23. As cited above, p. 251.

24. *A Thousand Plateaus*, as cited above, p.277.

25. p.83, Emily Bronte, *Wuthering Heights*, London: Random House, 2008.

26. Translated from Gilles Deleuze and Felix Guattari, *Milles Plateaux*, p.229, Paris: Les Editions de Minuit, 1980.

27. pp. 104-105, Carlos Castaneda, *The Eagle's Gift*, New York: Washington Square Press, 1991.

28. *The Chronicles of Thomas Covenant*, as cited above, p.758.

29. As cited above, p.743.

30. As cited above, p. 758.

31. pp. 54-55, Virginia Woolf, *The Waves*, London: Penguin, 1992.

32. pp.313-314 *The Norman Conquest*, Marc Morris, London: Windmill Books, 2013.

33. p. 186, Geoffrey of Monmouth, *The History of the Kings of Britain*, Woodbridge: The Boydell Press, 2007.

34. The term "ecumenon" has been taken from *A Thousand Plateaus* (see pp.50-56, as cited above), although here the concept is more narrowly defined.

35. *Thus Spoke Zarathustra*, as cited above, p.184.

36. As cited above, pp. 244-245.
37. As cited above, p.244.
38. As cited above, p. 289.
39. *Difference and Repetition*, pp. 89-90, as cited above.
40. *A Thousand Plateaus*, as cited above, p. 202
41. As cited above, p. 239.
42. As cited above, p. 286.
43. Virginia Woolf, "The Sun and the Fish," p. 189, *Selected Essays*, ed. David Bradshaw, Oxford: Oxford University Press, 2009.
44. *A Thousand Plateaus*, as cited above, p. 23.
45. pp. 277-278, William Gibson, *Neuromancer*, London: Victor Gollancz, 1995.
46. p. 282, Carlos Castaneda, *Tales of Power*, London: Penguin, 1990.

Contemporary culture has eliminated both the concept of the public and the figure of the intellectual. Former public spaces – both physical and cultural – are now either derelict or colonized by advertising. A cretinous anti-intellectualism presides, cheerled by expensively educated hacks in the pay of multinational corporations who reassure their bored readers that there is no need to rouse themselves from their interpassive stupor. The informal censorship internalized and propagated by the cultural workers of late capitalism generates a banal conformity that the propaganda chiefs of Stalinism could only ever have dreamt of imposing. Zer0 Books knows that another kind of discourse – intellectual without being academic, popular without being populist – is not only possible: it is already flourishing, in the regions beyond the striplit malls of so-called mass media and the neurotically bureaucratic halls of the academy. Zer0 is committed to the idea of publishing as a making public of the intellectual. It is convinced that in the unthinking, blandly consensual culture in which we live, critical and engaged theoretical reflection is more important than ever before.

ZERO BOOKS

If this book has helped you to clarify an idea, solve a problem or extend your knowledge, you may like to read more titles from Zero Books. Recent bestsellers are:

Capitalist Realism Is there no alternative?
Mark Fisher
An analysis of the ways in which capitalism has presented itself as the only realistic political-economic system.
Paperback: November 27, 2009 978-1-84694-317-1 $14.95
£7.99. **eBook:** July 1, 2012 978-1-78099-734-6 $9.99 £6.99.

The Wandering Who? A study of Jewish identity politics
Gilad Atzmon
An explosive unique crucial book tackling the issues of Jewish Identity Politics and ideology and their global influence.
Paperback: September 30, 2011 978-1-84694-875-6 $14.95
£8.99. **eBook:** September 30, 2011 978-1-84694-876-3 $9.99 £6.99.

Clampdown Pop-cultural wars on class and gender
Rhian E. Jones
Class and gender in Britpop and after, and why 'chav' is a feminist issue.
Paperback: March 29, 2013 978-1-78099-708-7 $14.95
£9.99. **eBook:** March 29, 2013 978-1-78099-707-0 $7.99 £4.99.

The Quadruple Object
Graham Harman
Uses a pack of playing cards to present Harman's metaphysical system of fourfold objects, including human access, Heidegger's indirect causation, panpsychism and ontography.
Paperback: July 29, 2011 978-1-84694-700-1 $16.95 £9.99.

Weird Realism Lovecraft and Philosophy
Graham Harman
As Hölderlin was to Martin Heidegger and Mallarmé to Jacques
Derrida, so is H.P. Lovecraft to the Speculative Realist philoso-
phers.
Paperback: September 28, 2012 978-1-78099-252-5 $24.95
£14.99. **eBook:** September 28, 2012 978-1-78099-907-4 $9.99 £6.99.

Sweetening the Pill or How We Got Hooked on Hormonal Birth
Control
Holly Grigg-Spall
Is it really true? Has contraception liberated or oppressed women?
Paperback: September 27, 2013 978-1-78099-607-3 $22.95
£12.99. **eBook:** September 27, 2013 978-1-78099-608-0 $9.99 £6.99.

Why Are We The Good Guys? Reclaiming Your Mind From The
Delusions Of Propaganda
David Cromwell
A provocative challenge to the standard ideology that Western
power is a benevolent force in the world.
Paperback: September 28, 2012 978-1-78099-365-2 $26.95
£15.99. **eBook:** September 28, 2012 978-1-78099-366-9 $9.99 £6.99.

The Truth about Art, Reclaiming quality
Patrick Doorly
The book traces the multiple meanings of art to their various
sources, and equips the reader to choose between them.
Paperback: August 30, 2013 978-1-78099-841-1 $32.95 £19.99.

Bells and Whistles More Speculative Realism
Graham Harman
In this diverse collection of sixteen essays, lectures, and interviews
Graham Harman lucidly explains the principles of Speculative
Realism, including his own object-oriented philosophy.

Paperback: November 29, 2013 978-1-78279-038-9 $26.95
£15.99. eBook: November 29, 2013 978-1-78279-037-2 $9.99 £6.99.

Towards Speculative Realism: Essays and Lectures Essays and Lectures
Graham Harman
These writings chart Harman's rise from Chicago sportswriter to co founder of one of Europe's most promising philosophical movements: Speculative Realism.
Paperback: November 26, 2010 978-1-84694-394-2 $16.95
£9.99. eBook: January 1, 1970 978-1-84694-603-5 $9.99 £6.99.

Meat Market Female flesh under capitalism
Laurie Penny
A feminist dissection of women's bodies as the fleshy fulcrum of capitalist cannibalism, whereby women are both consumers and consumed.
Paperback: April 29, 2011 978-1-84694-521-2 $12.95
£6.99. eBook: May 21, 2012 978-1-84694-782-7 $9.99 £6.99.

Translating Anarchy The Anarchism of Occupy Wall Street
Mark Bray
An insider's account of the anarchists who ignited Occupy Wall Street.
Paperback: September 27, 2013 978-1-78279-126-3 $26.95
£15.99. eBook: September 27, 2013 978-1-78279-125-6 $6.99 £4.99.

One Dimensional Woman
Nina Power
Exposes the dark heart of contemporary cultural life by examining pornography, consumer capitalism and the ideology of women's work.
Paperback: November 27, 2009 978-1-84694-241-9 $14.95
£7.99. eBook: July 1, 2012 978-1-78099-737-7 $9.99 £6.99.

Dead Man Working
Carl Cederstrom, Peter Fleming
An analysis of the dead man working and the way in which
capital is now colonizing life itself.
Paperback: May 25, 2012 978-1-78099-156-6 $14.95
£9.99. **eBook:** June 27, 2012 978-1-78099-157-3 $9.99 £6.99.

Unpatriotic History of the Second World War
James Heartfield
The Second World War was not the Good War of legend. James
Heartfield explains that both Allies and Axis powers fought for
the same goals - territory, markets and natural resources.
Paperback: September 28, 2012 978-1-78099-378-2 $42.95
£23.99. **eBook:** September 28, 2012 978-1-78099-379-9 $9.99 £6.99.

Find more titles at www.zero-books.net